NOT OF THIS WORLD:

FROM CUBAN REFUGEE

TO AMERICAN DREAM

TO FINDING GOD

786956

FROM RAGS, TO RICHES... TO RAGS—AGAIN!

As a young boy, Aurelio F. Barreto III fled communist Cuba with his family to search for the American Dream. But making his first million in his twenties only led the young inventor to realize he could not buy the kind of life he was searching for. Read what finally got Aurelio's attention, and how God used his life's failures and challenges in an unexpected new way.

TO MY FAMILY, AND OTHERS...

This book is dedicated first to my Lord and Savior Jesus Christ, Who died and rose for me and gave me life! I want to thank my wonderful wife Peggy, who has always loved me in spite of my many shortcomings and has always encouraged and supported me to go further in everything that I do. Peggy's positive attitude and consistent optimism have inspired me to move forward in spite of life's many challenges. God truly blessed me with Peggy as my lifelong partner who has always been faithful and steadfast. No matter what, I love Peggy.

To my wonderful children: CoLene, our oldest who was the first one in our family to place her faith and trust in Jesus Christ. I have always been blessed with her contagious enthusiasm, her ability to think clearly and discern quickly, and her overwhelming drive to do her best at everything. I thank my loving and gifted son Aurelio the IV ("JR") for his Godly wisdom, his awesome leadership skills and his consistent diligence to improve upon things. He is always there to listen to me. And to my highly creative Hilary, who has blessed me with her consistent love over the years. Hilary has helped me a lot during tough times. She is faithful to God in all she does, and has given me and our family years of laughter.

I also thank my parents, Sonia and Aurelio F. Barreto II, for sacrificing everything to bring me and my sister Sonia to the United States. They have both served as clear examples of hard working, responsible, and moral parents. And of course to my sister Sonia Barreto, for her contagious energy and enthusiasm, for always supporting my ideas, and for being a sister I can always count on.

To my spiritual mentor, Woodcrest Christian School Superintendent Randy Thompson, who not only brought me to the Lord in 1998 but also dedicated seven years after my conversion to disciple me in the Lord's Word. And to Pastor Milton Vincent from Cornerstone Fellowship Bible Church in Riverside, who taught me more about the gospel and the grace of Jesus than any other man. Milton has been a great instrument of God's grace in my life.

Last (but not least!) I thank Dr. Robert Jabs, whose idea it was to write this book. He was the first to see the potential of this story and had the vision to bring the initial writing together.

TABLE OF CONTENTS

Table of Contents

1: From nowhere to nowhere...2

2: Good times, bad times 10

3: The hole in the middle 16

4: To California with dreams...22

5: Train wreck 30

6: Piercing blue eyes in glasses 38

7: Chasing the American Dream 48

8: Dogging it...58

9: Finding the American Dream...68

10: Crossing the finish line...76

11: Called to the principal's office.......................................84

12: Into the light...96

13: By grace alone 106

14: By faith, not sight..120

15: The walls came tumbling down 132

16: In spite of circumstances 142

17: Trials of grace 156

18: The Lord is near 164

19: Jesus, my hope... 176

20: Loving God, loving others, trusting Him........................ 194

21: Never give up 206

22: Don't doubt, just believe................................... 212

23: Forever His!.. 220

Author's Note... 227

Appendix A: Salvation message................................ 229

Appendix B: A life-changing prayer........................... 233

Appendix C: Moving on; the Christian life.................... 236

Appendix D: A challenge for you – Part 1 242

Appendix E: A challenge for you – Part 2 250

Appendix F: Starting a business God's way 258

CHAPTER 1

FROM NOWHERE TO NOWHERE

*See, I am sending an angel ahead of you
to guard you along the way and to bring
you to the place I have prepared.*
(Exodus 23:20)

At age twenty-seven I started a business from the back of a pickup truck. We're talking about the Great American Dream here. My whole life I had enjoyed working, so I worked really hard. I worked really hard with my vending machine business, and I worked really hard at Dogloo. More about that later.

For now, it's enough to know that my Los Angeles-based company grew and grew. In fact, in just over ten years we were doing 62 million a year. Sixty-two million! That meant the company's earnings were a little bit over 8 million, and that was what the profits were, so we're talking a lot of money. And that wasn't just at the tenth year, either—we made a lot of cash very quickly.

So by the time I was thirty, I had made millions. That was my Great American Dream, right? Who wouldn't be excited about that kind of success? There I was with a big company of 600 employees, sales in 42 different countries and 200 different products. If you had seen me back then, you might have said…

That man's got it all.

But here's the thing: The more achievements I earned, the more stripes I put on my shoulder… the more depressed I got, and the more paranoid I became about losing it all. It was February 1996, my thirty-seventh birthday. It should have been a special time for me and I should have felt like celebrating. Despite all that, I just couldn't get out of bed because I had questions that were eating at me; questions I just couldn't answer.

Basic questions, like: Who am I? Where am I going? Is there any purpose behind all this? Why am I on this earth in the first place, and with so much pain? If I were to die right now, would I go to heaven? Was I good enough?

Well, I didn't have a lot of answers. But by that time I had a wonderful family—a wife and three kids. I was what you would call a "moral" man, too. Because by this time in my life, I wasn't into sex and I wasn't into drugs. In fact, many people probably said something like, "Aurelio? He sure does a lot of good things. He's always helping people. He's a great guy."

But that was what people saw on the surface. On the inside, I was empty. Totally and completely empty. And the worst part was I didn't have a clue how to change. Because all my life, all I knew how to do was to work hard and earn what I could. That was the path my parents set for me, ever since I was a little kid back in Cuba, back in 1967…

Sure, I was only seven at the time—but I knew we were in trouble. I could tell by the sound of the interrogator's voice, the slam of his hand on the table. We could hear him through the wall, even, as he grilled my dad in the next room.

"What are you taking with you? Why do you want to leave Cuba?"

Questions like that. Over and over. Everyone out in the waiting room could hear the Cuban official interrogating my father, trying to get him to change his mind and stay. Even today it's tough to think back on. As Dad was being questioned, my Mom, my four-year-old sister Sonia and I waited and waited with a room full of other families in that large waiting room with the high ceiling.

I looked around, trying to see other friendly faces, but to me everyone was a stranger. Still, we did have something in common, because everybody was there for the same reason: We were all waiting for freedom.

Meanwhile, the questions went on and on, and I could hear that Dad was wearing down. They accused him. They demanded answers. They bullied him. And they asked the same questions, a hundred different ways. Once in a while the interrogator would slam his palm on the table again, and we would all jump.

Even though I was pretty young in 1967, I could still recall the kind of fear that filled our waiting room. Even when they let Dad go for a few moments, they would yank him right back into the interrogation room to question him one more time. Would this ever stop?

Every time Dad returned to us, he looked as if his spirit had been crushed all over again. And I could tell things weren't going well just by looking at the deep worry lines on Mom's face.

One of the only bright spots I remember from that time was when one of my dad's business friends stepped over to say hello—and offered me a Lifesaver. I'd never eaten the American candy before; I hardly knew what to do with it. I held it up and stared through the hole in the middle, then finally popped it in my mouth.

"Wow, this is great!" I told my mother, sucking all the flavor I could out of the candy. "Have you tried this?" Well, she had. And more than that, she reminded me, this would be the kind of thing we would find in America—all the time.

I can still taste that first Lifesaver, and I still remember what it did for me at a time when I was starting to doubt if this America was worth all the trouble. That little candy with the hole in it helped me think that yes, maybe it was.

Still we waited. And for a seven-year-old it seemed like forever.

But somehow, finally, we were given a reluctant pass to go! So at the end of that long day we didn't waste any time jumping on the ancient bus that would take us from Havana to a small airport in Varadero Beach, where we would board an airplane for Miami, Florida.

But we weren't free just yet, and I could tell the people around me on the bus weren't quite ready to celebrate, either. Why else would so many people be crying? In between tears they sat like statues, dozing and waking during the long bus ride, hardly moving. Every once in a while, I heard coughing and sniffling. Some whispered to each other, others kind of whimpered. But nobody could sleep; the seats were too hard and the ride too bumpy. Mostly they just sat there, staring straight ahead, clutching a small bag of belongings that had been packed in a hurry the morning before.

My father stared out his window all night, yet there was nothing to see, only darkness. My little sister Sonia kept begging my mom to stop the bus and take her to the bathroom.

"Just a little farther," my mother promised her. *"Un poquito más..."*

Which meant nothing to a four-year-old. Sonia squirmed in her seat, trying to hold what a four-year-old can't. I stared out the window like my dad, since I couldn't sleep, either. My mind was racing and my body ached for rest, but I couldn't rest. Not yet. And the dark night seemed to hide us as the old bus lurched and bumped toward the airstrip.

We had to leave everything behind. My mom knew they wouldn't even allow her to take her wedding ring, so she slipped it off and left it behind. That was the first price she would pay for her family's ticket to freedom.

In my hand I held a small toy truck so tightly that it made a red imprint on my little hand. But I didn't care. I couldn't let it go; it was all I had left. The memory of that night would remain with me for a long time.

"Only one toy?" I had asked my mom the night before. What was she talking about?

"Only one," she told me, and the expression on her face convinced me she meant it. "We're packing and leaving tomorrow morning… for America."

America? Even more of a shock. Mom and Dad had never mentioned leaving for the U.S., not even in private. The last thing we would ever think to do was to talk about America in public, where others could hear. Who knew the kind of trouble that could bring?

And now we were leaving for Miami, Florida. I shivered at how my life had changed so drastically, so suddenly without any warning.

But my parents weren't kidding. Between the four of us, we had packed one suitcase full of clothes. And my sister and I were allowed to bring one toy. How to choose? In a panic I ran to my room to gaze at all the toys I had to choose from. I grabbed the biggest truck I had and hurriedly brought it back to my mother.

"No, Aurelio," she said. "It's too big."

It took a few more trips back to my room to pick out a toy that she would finally allow me to bring. In the end it wasn't the big truck I wanted but a small red truck that I could hold in my hand.

We had left early that morning, with no goodbyes and no ceremonies. We just got in the car and drove away; leaving behind my storehouse of treasures in the house I had grown to love and a country that had been my home. As we drove towards the interrogation room I stared at the little red truck in my hand, the same one I would clutch on the bus ride to come to the U.S.

I guess it was a symbol of my life in Cuba, and my only reminder of how ideal my life had once been...

CHAPTER 2

GOOD TIMES, BAD TIMES

When times are good, be happy; but when times are bad,
consider: God has made the one as well as the other.
(Ecclesiastes 7:14)

My childhood in Cuba had seemed ideal. Even though the crisis there had been simmering for a long time, I think in the early years a lot of Cubans secretly hoped Castro wouldn't last, or that someone else would elbow him out of power. But of course, that would not happen.

My family's business was cattle breeding, but my Dad's interests also drew him into a career in law. In fact, Dad knew Castro from the university where he was studying law. When my dad was a freshman, Fidel was a senior. He remembers the future dictator had a photographic mind. Fidel would rarely attend his law classes and he would miss most of the lectures, yet would get all A's on his tests. He was brilliant.

After Havana University, Dad ran into Castro during a cattleman's convention in Mexico City. He asked Castro how he was doing, and Castro asked for his help. Castro was then in exile, several years before the revolution against the dictatorship of Batista. Dad took a collection for Castro at the cattleman's convention, raising a couple thousand dollars at the time. But he never saw Castro again— at least not in person. Even then, the future dictator would shape the life of our family forever, and in ways we could never imagine.

Only a few years after the Mexico City encounter, Castro gained control of Cuba and betrayed his people by forcing communism on our nation. This was a horrific surprise to everyone. And as the state began to control everything, our lives turned into a living nightmare.

First, the new government began confiscating businesses, bank accounts and private assets. Savings accounts were frozen or transferred to the state. In the process, all the wealth my parents had accumulated—through sacrifice and hard honest work—was confiscated. They watched helplessly as the promise of democracy faded into a rigid, communist dictatorship. Human rights started to disappear, one by one. And like thousands of other professional Cubans, my dad lost his job and was assigned to another working for the new government as a driver. Before I was born, Dad was a successful businessman. By the time we left Cuba, Dad was driving a cab. A clear example of socialist redistribution.

But me? As a child, I had no clue of the tragedy unfolding around me. I was sheltered from reality.

I remember days when my friends and I would play on the mango trees. We always won the battle, always slayed the enemy as we played soldiers in my backyard. And we would play until we flopped down, exhausted, to watch the clouds that always reminded us of puffy, bright white elephants or rabbits against a brilliant blue sky. The Caribbean trade winds over the small island kept our skies blue and the weather perfect—or mostly so. Back then, nearly everything seemed perfect.

Every day when I got home from school my nanny would be there to greet us. She looked after Sonia and me as we grew up. We enjoyed the kind of childhood that included family get-togethers and family vacations every few months. We especially loved getting away to our beach house in Santa Jacinto, on the southern coast of the island, only a few feet from the ocean.

The beach house. I remember how sea breezes blew gently through our windows, which were always left open, night and day. We took long bike rides, and we spent hours exploring the shore. And the huge fish cookouts! We would catch angelfish by day off our boat dock, then go out at night with flashlights to find crabs and chase each other.

As kids, we couldn't imagine a better life. We loved the old Cuba, the Cuba that is still etched in my best memories. America? It was still a fuzzy dream; a land far away, a place filled with an abundance of things like Wonder Bread, grapes and 7-Up. Things that were no longer available in Cuba once Castro took over.

The years that we remained in Cuba waiting to leave, we saw the gradual disappearance of many things we were accustomed to, like grapes, sliced bread and soda. Essentials like rice, beans, and plantains were the only things in abundance the first year after Castro took power.

We did get American grapes a couple of times, though, around Christmas time. My grandmother meticulously peeled the skins and handed a handful of grapes to me; each person in my family only received a handful grapes. And as I studied the cool fruit, my mouth started to water. I wanted to pop all of them in my mouth at the same time, but I ate them one at a time to make them last.

I could think of nothing better—except maybe an American soda to wash it all down. In the days after Castro, for a rare treat we would sometimes get a case of 7-Up. Talk about exciting! Before we opened the top, everyone would just gather around to stare at a bottle, giving it a good once-over. Then we'd open it up, lean in to listen to the fizz, and smile. Oh, and the first sip, when the bubbles tickled my throat—ahhh, heaven! This was what the Americans drank.

Those days we talked about America once in a while, but not with any sense of envy. Sure, the Americans had nice food, but so did my Grandma Lola. At a lot of family gatherings, Grandma would serve delicious smoked sweet hams. Nothing was better than Sunday brunch at Grandma's, with steaming seafood and rice. So I had plenty of great memories in Cuba—especially of my family, and of the great times when we all got together.

Growing up, I could always count on getting together with big groups of cousins, aunts and uncles—as well as family gatherings like marriages, birthdays, graduations, and holidays. We were very close. Who worried? We could tell there was always so much love at each gathering. I felt like part of something much bigger than myself. As children, we would go out and play for hours, exploring, pretending, dreaming.... But it was the feeling of security and those joy-filled days that I remember most. A part of me wishes those days would have never ended.

As I grew older, though, everything started to change. After Castro took over we didn't dare speak of the United States anymore. Our large family wasn't able to meet as much, anymore either. And forget about any of the American delicacies. Under Castro, food rationing meant that every time we went to the store we only came back with the same three items: rice, beans and plantains.

But I never knew how closely everyone was being watched—or how it affected our lives—until one day, shortly before we eventually left Cuba, when my grandmother Lola had somehow found a ham. Amazing! It had been months, perhaps years, since we had enjoyed ham. And that special meal brought back the pleasure of sweeter times. It was more than delicious, and I went outside to enjoy a plateful in the evening's cool breeze. But I'd hardly stepped outside when my mother waved me back inside, as if I was doing something wrong. The urgency in her voice stopped me, but still I groaned a protest. Why did I have to hurry back inside? What was the panic?

"Because, Aurelin!" she told me (using my nickname), "if people find out we have a ham, your father will get thrown into prison."

My mouth dropped open, and that's when I started to understand what was happening: The peace and security of my childhood was gradually being torn away and replaced with uncertainty and secrecy. And this was just the start. We watched what we said. Soon we couldn't travel freely, and we would never return to our beloved beach house. Bit by bit the devil was stealing paradise. And as he so often does in life, at first it was barely noticeable. Like... no more ham dinners.

Before I knew what had happened, though, the pace of change quickened. Things got worse. But God wasn't just standing back and watching. Even if I couldn't see it then, He had already waded into the middle of the action. His hand was leading us toward a new country... and a new life.

CHAPTER 3

THE HOLE IN THE MIDDLE

Naked I came from my mother's womb, and naked I will depart.
The LORD gave and the LORD has taken away; may
the name of the LORD be praised.
(Job 1:21)

Suddenly the bus came to a huffing, squealing stop and I was jarred out of my remembering, back into the present—to 1967. From the endless interrogation, the monotonous ride had come to a halt outside a small airport. Well, at least we'd made it this far. Gradually everyone struggled from their seats, stretched their aching muscles, and made their way off the bus. Tired and anxious people who had been sitting for hours now jockeyed for position with their carry-on belongings and small children.

But my mother gently tugged my hand and smiled down at me as if to say, "It's going to be fine." In the mad scramble, though, I had no way of knowing. She looked at my father and reached for my sister, and I could only hold on to my little truck—and my mother. Well, we'd left everything else behind, even our friends and our large family. And we had no guarantee we'd see any of them again.

My final memory of Cuba was when I looked back at the small airport as we boarded the plane. The weather was sunny with a cool breeze that blew the skirt of my mom's dress. As we left the airport, Daddy shook hands solemnly with some friends he'd recognized in the boarding area, the way you might do at a funeral.

"Let's keep moving," he said as he urged us toward the waiting aircraft. I didn't need the sad look in my dad's eyes to tell me, though. We all knew this was a one-shot deal. We all knew we would never return.

In the next moment we went from a crowded airport to an even more crowded airplane cabin, and I choked on the stale air as we pushed our way to find open seats. But then no one said a word as the airplane lurched onto the runway. Even Mom and Dad white-knuckled the arms of their seats and the fear on their faces made my stomach churn. And though I could have wished for something to eat, I knew then it was good I hadn't. I couldn't eat. I couldn't close my eyes. My mind still raced.

And I couldn't help but think of Grandma Lola. When would I feel my grandmother's warm arms around me again? Maybe my mother guessed what I was thinking as she reached across and grabbed my hand, giving me a reassuring smile. I almost cried at this point, as tears filled my eyes. Did we really have to go? Why couldn't we find our way back to the beach house? Couldn't we just call everybody and have another family dinner? When would I ever get to lay my face on the cold marble floors and just watch the clouds?

My father might have watched the clouds, but from a different perspective. And when the airplane at last left the ground I think he finally relaxed, slumping back in his seat. It looked to me as if he had aged ten years in just a few days. All around me I could hear the sighs and the muffled cries of relief as the plane continued to ascend.

Now we were really on our way to America. This plane would take us to a new land of freedom of choice, human rights, and democracy. As for me, a seven year old boy, this meant a land of Wonder Bread, grapes and 7-Up. But even the thought of owning my own package of Lifesavers candy couldn't fill the hole in my heart. It was as if someone had ripped me out of a nice warm bed and thrown me out into a cold, dark night. I wasn't sure where I was going or if I would ever return to the security I'd known before.

Still we flew on. And as we approached Miami I was awestruck by the size of the buildings. Why would they need such big buildings? Eventually I would find out. But first we had to land, and they had to process us through another set of plain, intimidating rooms. Oh, and it was just like a roller coaster ride—as soon as you began to relax, the ride would pull you to yet another hill. I could almost taste the sick sense of fear once again as I glanced up at my mother's pale, drawn face. Tears rimmed her eyes. She must have struggled to keep her composure as we trooped along with all the other refugees.

Even though we'd landed in Miami, something was still wrong. Though I was too young to understand the depth of it all, I knew this nightmare was not over.

And so the questions flew through my mind once more. Could we be forced to return to Cuba? Would they really not let us into this country, after all? I stumbled and almost fell when the dread seemed to overtake me, but Dad grabbed my arm. We kept walking down a hallway in silence, our footsteps echoing on the linoleum floors. Dad lugged our large suitcase while Mom cradled Sonia in her arms. How much more could we take?

The man led us a short distance to a small room, which felt just like the one we'd left in Havana. The rooms were all the same. But that's where the similarity ended. The Americans gave us steaming hot chocolate and doughnuts. The doughnuts were sweet soft bread with a light coating of sugar that danced on your tongue before disappearing. And the hot chocolate warmed my insides. I'd never tasted either treat before, but I could definitely get used to this.

Then the roller coaster hit another bump, as an American customs official came in and started asking Dad tough questions. The inspector showed him intelligence pictures of dad getting into his car and pictures of him at work in Cuba.

"Is this you?" asked the man, waving the photo. "Is this your car?" My dad told us later how amazed he was. This official knew what car my dad drove and where he worked! How could these people know so much in 1967? I couldn't breathe or think. And for the next few hours I feared that they were going to take my father away or make us go back to Cuba.

During all this time no one slept except Sonia. My mom hugged her as she napped on her lap. My parents talked a little when Dad returned from this latest interrogation, and he seemed worried about being detained longer. No one knew for sure if we would be released. Our plans for the immediate future were put on hold. But just as tears brimmed over in my moms' eyes once more, my dad gently reached over and took her hand. He didn't say anything. He just held her hand and looked at her.

My father probably didn't see how much his life was like Job's. Job of the Bible, a very wealthy man who owned livestock, property, and trading companies. Job lost everything except his own life. We knew uncertainty and loss, too. The difference? We had no unshakable faith to comfort us.

Even so, God was faithful to us. Although we couldn't see Him working in our lives, He was there with His guiding hand. Because after all the waiting and interrogations, after all the travel and loss, after all the tears and uncertainty—finally we were allowed to enter our new country.

Our first few days in the United States were a blur. We stayed at my uncle's house, where a never-ending stream of friends and well-wishers paraded in and out. We received plenty of advice, since my parents had a lot of big decisions to make. Meanwhile, my sister and I got lost in the confusion of people and all their important grown-up things to do. So while my parents were trying to re-assemble what was left of our lives, I escaped by watching TV.

My favorite show was Batman. I didn't need to know much

English to see what was going on with the battles, the outlandish costumes and of course the batmobile. My old, familiar world had turned upside down and very little in this new place seemed familiar, but this new show grabbed my attention and held it. Because no matter how desperate things got in Gotham City, Batman could fix the problem. He could save everyone. When things went bad the red phone would ring and Batman would save the day.

And in my fantasies, it wasn't Batman, but a small Cuban boy in that bat suit. A boy with superpowers who saved his family and friends. He didn't sit idly by while grumpy men questioned his father's integrity or his decision to move to America. This little Cuban boy conquered the villain, saved the day and vanished in an instant back to the security of his home in the bat cave. At least for an hour, while the program was still on.

But all too soon the show would end and I would be back to reality in a strange house and a strange world. And nighttime was the toughest. Too many cars; too much activity; too many things unknown. I couldn't sleep in the strange pull-out bed, couldn't stop all the thoughts and worries from racing through my head. I always had too many questions, and not enough answers.

What was going to happen to us? Not another overnight change? Where were we going? I had no idea at the time, but God was already there, already ahead of us.

CHAPTER 4

TO CALIFORNIA WITH DREAMS

Have I not commanded you? Be strong and courageous. Do not be terrified; do not be discouraged, for the LORD your God will be with you wherever you go.
(Joshua 1:9)

California, here we come! After three days in Florida, we were back on an airplane—this time flying across the U.S. to Los Angeles. We'd heard all about California, so I was expecting plenty of sunshine and warm breezes, just like back home in Cuba.

Surprise! I stepped off the plane right into a cold, gray day. What was this? It was never overcast like this in Cuba. And the hazy, miserable weather only reminded me of how far we were from home.

What's more, no one welcomed us to Los Angeles. Not that we'd expected a marching band, but a few friends would have been nice. The welcoming committee never showed. By that time our mood had turned as somber as the overcast day, and we headed to our new home in downtown Los Angeles. Our new home in America! Where to?

An old hotel which was a haven for drug addicts and prostitutes, that's where. Here we were starting our new life in a new city and with only $20 in my dad's wallet. When we got out of the cab to see our new place we almost had to hold our breath.

Garbage overflowed onto the sidewalk just outside the doors of the large brick building. The alley smelled worse than rotten food. Vagrants lay outside reeking of alcohol, their clothes stained and soiled. Inside wasn't any better.

Roaches skittered across dirty floors. My mom cried as she scrubbed the filth from the toilet in our bathroom. It was so thick she had to scrape it off with a spatula, but she went on crying and scraping, sobbing and scrubbing. What could I do to make her feel any better?

The next day, my mom went out and bought a small electric

burner to cook hot dogs: We had hot dogs for lunch and hot dogs for dinner. I tried my best not to think of what we'd left behind, especially Grandma Lola's wonderful cooking and the family feasts we used to enjoy.

But I couldn't help feeling homesick. The sound of sirens, traffic and people woke me up almost every morning. So early! Cuba was nothing like this. I missed the gentle island breezes and the carefree days back home. But what good did it do to miss what was so far gone?

The great news was my dad found work right away, so we only spent a week in the roach hotel. That was long enough. A friend of my dad's helped us move into an apartment in Inglewood, California. That's where Dad landed his first job in America, working as a janitor cleaning bathrooms at a motor home factory.

Welcome to the USA.

Imagine him, a trained lawyer, cleaning toilets! Dad obviously could have grumbled about losing everything and having to start over. Instead he always focused on the future.

"We're in the United States of America now," he would tell us, over and over. "Our new country, and they have been kind enough to let us live here. Our heritage is Cuba, yes. But we're Americans, now. And this America is the land of freedom and opportunity."

I wasn't so sure. And plenty of times I just didn't understand how it would all work out. I tried to follow his example, but mostly I had no idea how to keep up with this man. He'd get home late at night, grab a quick dinner and then bury himself in books. He wanted to become a U.S. citizen as soon as possible, and that would take some studying.

I remember watching him study at the dinner table long after dinner, night after night, hunkered over his books. And I wondered if things would ever be different—or when they'd finally be okay. Because after he finished studying to become a citizen, he studied to get his teaching credentials. All this studying! It seemed like a lot of work for something you couldn't hold in your hand or buy ice cream with.

And yet… this American dream of freedom, opportunity and success gripped my father in a way I could not ignore. I knew people risked their lives for this kind of dream, though I didn't always quite understand why. What was the big attraction? Mainly I was just glad to be with my parents and my sister in a place where Batman was still on TV.

My parents had no time for television. From the time we arrived in Los Angeles, Dad seemed to care mostly about just two things: paying the bills and chasing the future. He worked long and hard every day, seven days a week, until late at night, as he worked his way up into better and higher paying jobs.

But I didn't care so much about all that. I missed him. I never saw him. He would eat, study, and go sleep. And then he would start all over again, early the next day.

Mom worked and helped Dad at night, too. It seemed a little easier for her since she had graduated from college in the United States in her youth, and she spoke fluent English. But she still had to work hard. Mom and Dad were already on the job by the time we kids would wake up in the morning. And with both of them so busy, the apartment manager, Mrs. Cook, would often see me and Sonia safely to school.

At the time, I didn't understand what drove my parents, or how much energy it took them to keep moving. I had a hard time even getting up in the mornings. Even so, my dad managed to plant his ideals in me at a young age. So of course I had my own dreams, too. But I didn't dream of being the President of the United States, like a lot of my friends. I didn't want to write a great novel or grow up to become a famous actor. No, not me—I wanted to be in business. Even at the young age of seven, and having just arrived in America, I knew what I wanted.

So I didn't just want to outdo the boy next door; it didn't stop there. Being in business wasn't just my goal-it was to be a millionaire. I wanted to amass a fortune big enough so no one could take it away. Becoming a millionaire would be the ticket. It would bring me the security, prestige and happiness I wanted.

Or so I thought.

Anyway, I made myself a promise. My vow: make a million dollars by the age of thirty. Sure, it was a huge dream for a boy who had just emigrated here from Cuba, but I was one determined little guy. And I held on to the dream, even in the toughest of times.

At first we wore hand-me-down clothes and rummage sale shoes. We didn't have fancy new bikes or name brand clothes. We ate meals at home and played around the apartment... and survived. And before long we began to see ourselves as American as apple pie and Chevrolet.

Sonia and I did pretty well in school, too. We did as well as anyone, really. We learned the English language quickly. Yet I knew I was one of the "have-nots," and I was determined that would change.

It did, too—slowly at first. But over the next five years we were able to afford newer clothes and go out to eat, usually on a Friday evening. It was just a little hamburger joint, Dallas Palace I think, but it tasted like a five star restaurant. It wasn't just a night out for us. This was huge! And after we polished off the burgers, Sonia and I would beg Dad for an ice-cream cone. Please?

But no matter how many times we asked, Dad would just shake his head no; somehow ice cream was more than we could afford. So we were always left wanting more. Yet all around me I couldn't help noticing the well-to-do people with their big houses and nice cars, and I thought to myself,

Never mind ice cream. If only I could have those kinds of things, I'd be happy the rest of my life.

God didn't really figure too much into the picture. Not that I didn't have any knowledge of God growing up, but it was limited. So around the fifth or sixth grade, some of my friends told me about going to church, and I wanted to go, too. I wanted what they had, yet Mom wasn't sure of the kind of church my friends attended so she didn't allow me to go with them. She had grown up in a very ritualistic church upbringing, one that was based more on actions and routines than on faith and a personal relationship with God. On top of that, she had attended a private religious school in the States, a college in the East Coast where the nuns discouraged students from reading the Bible. She wanted time to decide about church.

So I didn't go. But deep down I knew I needed much more. Sometimes nightmares woke me in the middle of the night, familiar nightmares that I could never quite recall when I woke. I would feel the fear knotting my gut as tears fell from my eyes, and I was so scared I could hardly go back to sleep. I was afraid to even close my eyes. My mom would try to help with a prayer, and sometimes that would help a little. Even so, I knew something was missing, though back then I didn't know exactly what.

Now I know I needed the kind of peace that only Christ could have given me—but I'd still never heard the good news of Jesus. If I had, I might have steered clear of the heartache that was just about to knock me off my feet.

CHAPTER 5

TRAIN WRECK

As a dog returns to its vomit, so a fool repeats his folly.
(Proverbs 26:11)

I knew without a doubt what my parents expected of me. I understood their high standards. How could I not? But hey, now I was going to Hawthorne High—the party school, the surfer school, the same school the Beach Boys went to, ten years before. So pretty quickly my focus switched from getting good grades and pleasing my folks to… well, fitting into the party scene.

After all, up to that point in my American experience I'd never felt like I'd fit in. And now I wanted to—badly. I wanted to be one of the guys. I was tired of the loneliness, the emptiness. I thought that if I could just find my way into the "in" group, everything would be okay. So because I wanted to be doing what the cool kids were doing, I started going to the same parties the cool kids went to. I wanted to be accepted; we all do.

It's not hard to guess what happened next: first the drinking, then the smoking, then the snorting. When alcohol started to lose its magic punch, I looked for other highs in marijuana and cocaine. Sometimes I didn't even know why I was doing it. But eventually I would get high in the morning, high at lunch, high in the evening. Before, during and after school, all the way through most of high school.

One of the big hangouts that summer of 1975 was the Manhattan Beach Pier. We could take a bus there from Hawthorne, about five miles from the beach. If we were lucky we'd snag a dollar to buy a pizza and a Coke at Zeppy's. At another place just off the beach we could get a burger for 30 cents, fries for 14 cents, and a malt for 25 cents. Okay, so this sounds like a lot of "Happy Days" memories, but the Pier was definitely the Cheap Date Capital of area, besides being the center of our summertime fun.

Summer eventually melted into fall, though, which meant I had to return to school for my junior year. My grades continued to slip and although I thought I could hide it fairly well, I was still drinking and using drugs. For the time being, I found acceptance with my stoner friends. Even though I wasn't sure who I was, I thought I fit in—for now.

In fact, sometimes drugs would help me escape. For a while I thought they gave me a feeling of peace and security, a feeling that I could stop running from my loneliness. But by this time getting high had become the center of my life. Eventually I didn't focus on goals, didn't achieve anything, just did everything I could to try to fill that nagging hollowness inside of me. I was probably still looking for the paradise I thought I'd left behind in Cuba, back when life felt secure and happy. I never really found it, of course.

Eventually the drugs dragged me to a place where my life began to spin out of control. I began feeling depressed and paranoid, which led me to make more and more dumb choices. The incredible part was, through it all I kept telling myself I had time. Plenty of time to get my act together, tomorrow or maybe next month. No worries. Right! In real life my grades had crashed and burned, and I ran out of time. Even my family could tell something was seriously wrong with me, so I avoided home as much as I could and stayed out later and later with my friends.

I couldn't keep running from the truth, though. By then I knew that the drugs were only making me feel worse—about myself and my life. They didn't help me fill that void inside myself. I didn't even know why I was doing them anymore. The process of getting high was better than actually being high. But that didn't stop me. And one afternoon while getting high with my friends, we got caught with a pound of pot. Dad had to pick me up in jail.

At first Dad was so quiet, the silence killed me. I could almost hear my heart beating as I groped for excuses to explain what I'd been doing. Of course I didn't really have anything to say.

"Dad..." I mumbled, feeling numb. "I'm—"

"I don't want to hear it, Aurelio," he interrupted. "What right do you have to throw your life away?"

He wasn't expecting an answer as he lashed out at me.

"Is this why we moved to a new country? For you to waste your life in drugs and throw away your opportunity for something good? Is this what I've been working so hard to give you? Now look at you."

I didn't want to. All I could see was my dad, his face cherry red by this time. Still I couldn't speak.

"Do you know what you're doing, Aurelio? Do you understand?"

Not really, not yet. But I would. Meanwhile he gripped his head in his hands and shook his head violently, repeating "No!" over and over as if I had died. In a way maybe I had. I was still paralyzed. So I just sat there, speechless.

And it still hurts me today to think how badly I had hurt and humiliated my father that afternoon. My arrogance and stupid choices cut to the heart of this hard-working, moral man. He'd already been through so much.

So the good news was that this confrontation helped me see how much I was hurting other people by what I was doing. My dad, especially. And really, when I started to get an honest look at things it didn't take long to figure out that getting high wasn't filling the emptiness I felt. It wasn't really making me feel like I fit in anywhere, either. In the end all it did was make me sick, and I knew that I wanted to get off this train before it wrecked.

Or maybe it already had—but now it didn't matter. By God's grace I now had a chance to see my father in a different light, and I no longer resented him working the long hours. After walking around in shock for a few days, I started to understand all the things he had done for my sister and me. I began to see why my parents worked and sacrificed to give us a better life. And slowly I started to change, started to change directions. I started meeting other friends, and I began to work on getting my grades up. It looked as if my life had taken a turn for the better.

I actually did love to work. I found jobs when possible. My earliest recollection of working hard came from my Uncle Gaspar. My uncle was not an intellectual type like my dad, but a huge figure of a man. A very strong man. I started tagging along with Uncle Gaspar when I was about ten years old. He would bring me along to house cleaning jobs, and to also paint old apartments that he would do on the weekends. The work was extremely hard and filthy at times, but even so it was a chance to work with my great Uncle Gaspar. I learned to work hard and put in a full day's work. I would get home exhausted, and then quickly fall asleep.

I still miss my uncle a lot. He considered me like his own son, and loved me like one. He passed away to be with the Lord years ago, but I will always remember his cheerful encouraging laugh, and his great love for me.

Later on in junior high, I also worked for Sheriff Hayes. Everyone called him "Big Red." Red owned a few apartments in town and I would help him out as well. It was Red who also scolded me when I got caught smoking pot.

While in high school, in spite of the party scene and all the distractions, I was fortunate enough to often work 40-plus hours per week and go to school at the same time. I had started working in tenth grade at a local grocery store, the Rockview Dairy. I began as a stock boy and managed to work my way up to cashier. My manager, George, taught me to be honest and to always keep my word; to do what I said I would do, and on time.

Getting back to my "other" life, the life of doing drugs… I knew I had to quit, and eventually I did. Quitting drugs, though, didn't change my basic problem: I was still dead inside. Empty. So the only thing I could think to do was to look for yet another way to fill my emptiness. Not drugs, this time, but girls. I thought, *If only I can date the prettiest girl in the school, if I could just have the prettiest girl, then I'll feel like somebody, for sure.*

That didn't work, either. By then I was a senior in high school. I had tried drugs and sex countless times but neither one could fill that void in my life.

At age eighteen, I felt like I was at the end of the line. Honestly, I was ready to commit suicide! Nothing that I'd tried worked for me. Today it reminds me of King Solomon's words: *"Yet when I surveyed all that my hands had done and what I had toiled to achieve, everything was meaningless, a chasing after the wind; nothing was gained under the sun."* (Ecclesiastes 2:11)

After countless failed relationships, I might even have agreed with Solomon at the time—if I'd known anything about the Bible. Because without God, everything truly *was* meaningless. Here's where God's grace kicked in, though, once more—this time in a hospital kitchen.

I'm glad I worked during my senior year; this time though, it was washing dishes in a hospital. That's where I met George, a fellow dishwasher. Pausing from his work one day, he had a few words of advice that would help change my life.

"Aurelio, you have too much potential." He stared straight at me. "You don't want to end up like me, washing dishes for the rest of your life. You have got to get out of here."

For the second time that year I was in total shock. The first time, of course, had been when my father took me home from jail. Now this old broken man seemed to be able to see straight down to my soul, and I knew he was right. I had to get out of there—somehow.

So once again I turned back to what I knew, what I'd been taught. I turned back to doing things right. I turned back to my old dream of becoming a millionaire. That would be my ticket out, once I graduated—if I graduated. I vaguely remember school dances, math classes and bands like Led Zeppelin and Pink Floyd. Even today I have no idea how I ever graduated from high school.

I can't forget the steadying influence of my parents, though. My dad and mom were the hammers who stopped me from wasting my life in drugs and going down the wrong road. I also remember the growing drive I started to feel around that time; the drive that awakened and pushed me to want to start my first business. *Rich people are always smiling*, I thought. *Someday soon, that's going to be me.*

Maybe it *would* be me, despite all the bumps I would face ahead. All I knew was I needed something more in life, and in the back of my mind I also knew I needed God. I just didn't know yet where I would find Him, or what I would do if I did. I guess I still thought He'd be hiding in a stained glass window or behind an impressive altar somewhere. So I stopped at a church one day—Saint Joseph's in Hawthorne—full of hurt and confusion about the future. The typical 18-year-old stuff. I begged God for help and strength, and was shocked when I actually received it. That was basically my first encounter with God.

Yet God's help never seemed permanent, and my wimpy faith hung by a thread. I returned to the church a few times after that attempt at drive-by religion, but I would never pick up a Bible or study God's Word to learn more. So I never picked up the only kind of advice that could have helped change my life. Today I think of how the Apostle Paul warned new believers in one of his letters, saying that *"See to it that no one takes you captive through hollow and deceptive philosophy, which depends on human tradition and the basic principles of this world rather than on Christ."* (Colossians 2:8)

I wish I'd heard that advice when I was eighteen, because by this time I was well along on my next wild goose chase. Even though I was attending church now and then, I never truly gave my heart over to God. That only gave the devil many opportunities to distract me from the Truth. Setting goals, working hard, and getting ahead would occupy me from then on, for the next decade and beyond. These things became my new drug of choice.

And yet…God still had plans for me. Toward the end of my high school years, He began calling me to a different destiny. A week before high school graduation God would show me who was going to share that destiny with me.

CHAPTER 6

PIERCING BLUE EYES IN GLASSES

A wife of noble character who can find?
She is worth far more than rubies.
(Proverbs 31:10)

Peggy Vincent had to be one of the prettiest girls in Hawthorne High, and a straight-A student, besides. She'd been voted "Most Talented" in our class of 1977.

So why did this petite, red-haired beauty approach me and my buddy John that evening? We'd been sitting off in the corner of the Hermosa Beach dance club, watching couples dance. Surely she wasn't coming to ask one of us to...

"Would you dance with me?" She looked straight at me with her fabulous smile and those piercing blue eyes in her cute glasses. "Please?"

Who, me? I wasn't quite believing this, but I wasn't about to say "no," either. And as she led me out to the dance floor, she explained that she and her friend Carol were trying to ditch a couple of older men who had been pursuing them. They needed a diversion, and I was it.

Oh. That wasn't exactly what a guy would want to hear, but I couldn't help enjoying the dance, as well as the conversation. Who wouldn't enjoy being this close to Peggy? When the music stopped, though, she thanked me and headed back to her table.

"Wait! Uh..." It couldn't hurt to ask. Her friends were still entwined on the dance floor. "Do you want to sit down over here?"

Meaning, with John and me. Or mostly with me. She thought for a moment, but surprised me by saying yes. And that wasn't the end of the surprises, either. She actually talked with me, and laughed like an old friend. It was almost as if we fit together, right from the start. And as the evening went on we found out we had a lot in common, shared many of the same goals, came from the same kinds of working class families. We understood each other. I was sure from the start that I'd lost my heart to this girl.

What a night! My mind danced with questions. Was she for real? Was she serious? Could this work? Did she really think I was thoughtful and kind of cute? Well, she said I was. I could hardly sleep that night, thinking about this girl. And pretty soon we would get a chance to test this new relationship.

She had a lot to teach me about life, and about love. But first she had to teach me to drive a stick shift. Which I'd always wanted to learn because I'd always wanted a Volkswagen van. Besides, driving lessons would be a great excuse for spending time with Peggy. So I jumped in her Mazda without a clue of what to do.

"Just step on the gas," she told me, "and ease off the clutch."
Sounded easy enough. But my face turned pink as I jerked the car to a hiccup-halt once more while she tried to hide a giggle behind her hands.

"Let's try it again," she told me. "Only this time…"

I couldn't believe it. Her patience and encouragement intrigued me just as much as her dancing had the night before. And after I discovered the secret of driving a clutch, together we found more and more reasons to see each other. In fact, Peggy and I soon spent just about every free moment together. We loved driving to the beach, or up the coast to the lighthouse at Palos Verdes. We loved exploring, dreaming, talking about the future. And when I wasn't with Peggy, I was thinking about her.

Six months after we met on the dance floor, I knew exactly what I wanted. I didn't want to date anyone else. We had talked more seriously about our relationship, and I thought all the signs looked right for me to make the move. I wanted to marry Peggy Vincent. Why not ask her? Everything was going so well. I was sure it was the right time to propose. But when I pulled out the engagement ring I'd chosen for her...

"No, Aurelio." She sighed. "I can't marry you."What? Her words nearly knocked the breath out of me. Why not? "It scares me half to death," she went on. "I think we should date other people."

Was I hearing her right? Okay, I knew we were only eighteen, but we were both mature. Or I thought we were. I also knew Peggy's mother was on her fifth husband, so marriage had to be a pretty frightening proposition from Peggy's point of view.

"Aurelio..." she started, but I held up a hand to stop her. I'd heard enough, been hurt enough. "You can date me, and only me." I laid it down firmly enough so she couldn't mistake my meaning. "Or we're not together."

Didn't she understand? All my life I'd been searching for someone to accept me, to love me. And now when I'd finally found her, what could be wrong with asking her to stay with me? I thought she felt the same way about me, but now she struggled to explain.

"I'm scared," she told me. Scared? Me, too. Scared of losing her, of not being a whole person without her. "We're too young," she explained, "and with me going off to college..."I could think of ways to fix that, but she wouldn't change her mind. "I'm sorry, Aurelio."

Sorry? Me, too. I slipped the little ring box back in my pocket as I fought back tears. I couldn't swallow the lump of rejection in my throat, and I couldn't say a word as she grabbed my hand.

"Please understand..." Now she was crying. "I'm just not ready."

I didn't trust myself to speak, so I just stared at the floor. Really, I didn't have anything else to say. So a few days later she moved away to begin her college studies. And after a while we began to date other people. I went back to work.

Still, we saw each other a few times over the next six months— between her college classes, during school vacations and when I wasn't working. Every time, I thought she looked more beautiful than ever. And every time, my heart stopped at the sight of her, and I forgot about anyone else I'd dated. I could never say it, but I always wondered: Would there be any possibility of getting back together?

Maybe. Because over time her fear of commitment faded a bit, along with my hurt. We spent even more time together talking. I felt hopeful. She didn't let go when I held her hand. I couldn't know it then, but now I clearly see God's hand bringing us back together. It was like a gift. I remember telling her the day we both agreed to get back together that I had been a wreck without her. She looked into my eyes through her glasses and I knew once more what I had always known. I had a soft spot for girls in glasses, but Peggy was *the* one for me. No doubt, anymore. This was love!

Even so, I was careful not to mention marriage or commitment after we got back together. I just enjoyed having Peggy back. We talked. We laughed. We cried. Peggy eventually left college for a career opportunity at Hughes Aircraft. We both worked, and we focused on saving money. In fact, we really didn't take much time out of our busy schedules for anything other than work because we were planning for a solid financial future.

Meanwhile, God was waiting patiently for us to turn to Him. Oh, we knew about the Lord; we just didn't see how He had anything to do with our lives. We never read the Bible, so its message had no real place in our lives, our careers, or our relationship. Instead, we focused on stuff, on getting more. If I had two, I wanted three. And no matter how much we got, it was never enough.

Actually, Peggy did know some of God's peace in her life—sort of an echo from an experience she'd had as a child. Peggy's mother was a functioning alcoholic. And when Peggy was young, some nights she wondered if her mother would even make it home, if she might hurt or even kill someone by driving drunk. So one night when Peggy was about ten years old, she began to pray as she never had before: "Please Lord, please watch over my mother. Watch over her when she is driving home. I know you are my God, and you will take care of my mom and me."

It didn't stop there. From her bed Peggy cried out for the safety of those people her mother could run into on her way home. She pleaded with God, begged Him to guide her mother safely home. And though it was a heart-wrenching experience at the time, eventually Peggy felt a peace—even an audible voice telling her that "everything is going to be all right." Perhaps when we feel the most helpless, God reaches down to comfort us. Comforted, Peggy fell asleep—and her mother made it back without hurting herself.

What's more, that same peace stayed with Peggy, guiding her through high school and other tough times. Perhaps it helped bring her back to me after we split up. I didn't know for sure, and I didn't question it, since I was just satisfied to have her in my life once again.

The months slipped by, busy and filled with work and dreams. So when we were both twenty one we decided to buy a little 900-square-foot house at 914 South Eucalyptus street in Inglewood, not far from Los Angeles. Instead of spending money on a future honeymoon, we chose to sacrifice this luxury in order to invest in our first house. All we needed was five percent down, but still this decision was a big step for the two of us—and a big problem for my parents.

"Your mother made a few comments about us buying a house," Peggy told me one evening as we were finishing dinner. "She has a problem with us living together."

Nothing new there. My parents had already told me they weren't happy about our future living plans. It was my mom's Catholic upbringing. Even though she didn't go to church, she'd held onto some of the lessons she'd learned in church when she was young. She'd learned what was right, and what was wrong. And living together, she knew, was one of those taboos.

"So," Peggy continued, "I thought maybe it would be a good time to get married."

Had she said what I thought she said? I nearly fainted as she went on. "I mean, we're almost married, anyway." She waited for me to answer, to say something. Anything! I stared at her and she stared back at me. Finally I managed to choke out a few words.

"Sounds good to me."

Well, it did sound good. Real good. And that's all it took to kick off our wedding plans. The only problem was, buying a house and planning a wedding are two major events. Looking back, we probably shouldn't have tried to do both at the same time. But never mind. Peggy ran all over town, checking out details, meeting with dozens of people, and making sure everything would work on our slim budget. How would we be able to make it work—dress and all—for under $2,000?

So it was a crazy time, and some days we didn't see each other at all. Work pulled us apart, just as buying a house did. For that matter, so did planning a wedding. We just had too much on our "to do" lists. But all that major craziness came to a head on an overcast spring morning, April 26, 1980.

We'd heard the weather forecasts. Rain threatened to dump at any time, yet we'd planned an outdoor ceremony, just outside a little chapel in Inglewood. And though we'd tried to keep the wedding small, it had swelled to well over 200 guests. So that morning everyone was waiting for the bride to show, especially the nervous groom. And I had plenty to be nervous about. Because even after the wedding march started... no bride.

I wondered: Had Peggy changed her mind? Thank God, she did not. She stood just out of my line of sight with her father, Ralph, having a moment with him.

Ralph was a generous and calm man. As a brilliant engineer designing nuclear submarines for the Northrop Corporation, Ralph traveled the world as a respected and sought after consultant.

"Do you hear that?" her father asked her. "Hear what?" Peggy strained to hear what he was talking about, but couldn't hear a thing. "There. Hear it?" He asked her again, pausing just long enough. "It's my knees knocking."

Well, that did it. I wouldn't know about this little exchange until later, but Peggy's dad knew what his daughter needed. He helped her start this new life with a smile—and I appreciated it more than he could know.

From then on everything about the wedding went as planned. Or almost. At one point an overhead jet interrupted the ceremony, and guests held their ears until the roar passed by. I looked up at the gray and wondered if our skies would open up before the minister had a chance to declare us husband and wife.

It almost did. But God held off the rain until just minutes after the "I do." Showers poured down just as the ceremony ended, and we hurried through the rain to the Knights of Columbus hall for our reception.

Finally married! Finally legal! We had closed on the house and moved into our new place with my parents' blessing. Finally we could relax just a little. And actually, the jitters that had chased me through my teenage years did seem to slack off after the wedding. Just a little.

But the devil was not done with me yet, as I would find out soon enough.

CHAPTER 7

CHASING THE AMERICAN DREAM

Whoever loves money never has money enough;
whoever loves wealth is never satisfied with his income.
This too is meaningless.
(Ecclesiastes 5:10)

Strange. I was always really good at twisting God's grace into the kind of thing He never intended. For example: Straight out of high school, I landed a job as a draftsman for Rockwell International. My first big job!

As a kid, I would love to draw geometric pictures, and it was Peggy who one day suggested I look into drafting. Starting out on my first corporate job as a draftsman was the beginning of the second phase of my life.

It would become clear how work would eventually take over my life. But for now this was just a start. I attended El Camino College at night while working my day job and pushed hard to become the best draftsman I could be. I began to understand then what I still believe today, *"A man can do nothing better than to eat and drink and find satisfaction in his work. This too, I see, is from the hand of God."* (Ecclesiastes 2:24) I found that work was a good thing and that full time work would keep me out of trouble. And I also began to learn that to succeed I would have to focus on the big picture.

I learned about the big picture from my dad. The big picture meant looking first at the *why* in situations. Dad taught me that the *why* in situations was far more important than the *how*. Dad told me, "You can always find people that know *how* things work, but finding people that actually know *why* things are needed in the first place, is a rare thing."

That lesson served me well at North American Rockwell. I began to focus on the reasons behind challenges, the strategy behind things. When I understood the *why* behind a task, rather than just *how* things had always been done, I could often improve existing ideas and discover solutions that worked a whole lot better. So early on, I always knew I could find better solutions by looking at the problems from a different perspective. "That's how we've always done it" was never part of my vocabulary. This too was God's grace in my life.

So I charged ahead in my work, not always sure where I was going, but very much in a hurry to get there. If nothing else, I was determined. And though I didn't totally see what was going on in my younger years, I now understand God was in complete control of the details. I found favor back then for a reason, and the details are worth explaining to show how God's hand works.

Mentors. I was blessed with great mentors right from the start. Blair Reardon, my manager at Rockwell, was a brilliant engineer who enjoyed teaching and challenging me. In that kind of environment I enjoyed trying to deliver more than was expected. I also learned to tackle the big picture, first, and then watch the smaller steps take care of themselves—as long as I kept focused on the end result. It's almost a biblical approach, and I'm grateful for how each learning opportunity added something to who I am today as an entrepreneur and as a leader.

Over the following years, by God's grace, I worked to become a self-taught design engineer, doing freelance projects for companies such as Xerox Corp., Hughes Aircraft Company, and Mattel Toys. Under my mentor at Xerox, Bill MacCleod, I really learned how to design. He taught me to think creatively and solve problems, to look beyond the obvious. We worked on everything from gear trains and electronic packaging, to steel structures and plastics for high-speed computer printers. Bill also taught me that rules are merely made by men, and rules are to be actually improved upon. That was a new and exciting concept to me.

Building on my Rockwell experience, I learned to work a challenge, backwards. Start with the solution, then work backwards to get to the problem. That sounds strange but it was actually a great way to work. For one thing it helped me always to focus on the end result, the strategy on what I actually needed. It helped me put everything else into perspective, so I rarely got lost in the details or bogged down in smaller steps. We never wasted time at Xerox, and we never lost opportunities waiting around to collect all the answers. We always moved forward, and not sideways.

We worked hard, too—sometimes up to twelve hours a day, six days a week to finish projects. I remember having a cold once and telling Tom Booth, a friend and senior design engineer that I was going to call in sick.

"Why do that?" Tom said. "Can't you work through a cold?"

I thought, *Well, sure but...*

At first I was a little puzzled by his attitude. But when I really thought about it, sure, I could keep working. A cold didn't have to stop me from being productive, and that lesson helped me stay focused and driven even when I didn't feel physically at my best. Now that I'm in my fifties, I prefer investing in good, solid sleep instead of dragging through a virus.

I stayed awake for opportunities during this time, though. And when I was offered more money at Mattel Toys, I jumped at the offer. Here was another chance to get ahead, I thought. The work would be a little different, and challenging, too.

At Mattel I got a chance to grow as a consumer product designer, and I began to refocus my thinking on how people would look at new products. My boss, Bob Sterns, taught me the art of conceptualizing. He was a great teacher. We had to think everything through first, to form the ideas in our mind. That helped me improve my productivity, because I learned to recognize and visualize problems before they actually occurred.

Conceptualizing also helped me prove out solutions. Would the idea solve a problem, or would it actually create more problems? Would it help save money? Could it help take a good thing—and make it even better? My time at Mattel trained me to look for real-life, practical solutions, not just theories. The simplest of ideas are always the best of ideas.

But of course I was always moving on, so after a couple of years at Mattel, I accepted a contract with the Hughes Aircraft Corporation. From toys to rockets! In this environment, I had to bring all my skills in creative thinking, problem solving and visualization to a higher level. My boss there was Bill Tanabe—the toughest boss ever, but I respected him the most.

Bill put me to work on very complex high frequency radar systems. Here I really had to focus on the strategy, to concentrate on the goal, to think of the "why" before the "how." These skills would be priceless later on in business. I learned to use intuition and creativity while meeting goals… on time. Always on time. Bill pushed hard and always seemed to demand more from me than anyone else.

Funny, though: I didn't mind. In fact, I enjoyed his challenges and his powerful sense of urgency. This kind of pressure cooker helped sharpen my creative thinking and problem solving skills. Because at Hughes, it wasn't good enough just to find a new way to solve a problem; we needed results and efficiency—*yesterday.*

At Hughes I also learned a lot about how to lead, how to take charge, and how to take responsibility for my countless mistakes. Bill showed me how to tackle the biggest, thorniest problems without backing down. I even started to relish the challenge of an "impossible" goal. So my career was taking off at Hughes, but that only took me to a height where I could search for even more opportunities. Peggy and I had invested in our second home, and we'd even saved $25,000 on top of that. Later, we bought a triplex as an additional investment. When all our friends were going places and doing things, taking vacations and going on trips, we were working and scraping to get ahead. Work and save, work and save.

Peggy grew in stature also while working at Hughes Aircraft. She started in the payroll department at age eighteen, and quickly grew in knowledge and accomplishments. While Peggy was also self-taught, she achieved in her first ten years what normally took most people a lifetime. Later on, she advanced to become a top systems manager/analyst at Hughes, directing senior staff programmers and implementing countless complicated company systems. Actually, Peggy is twice as smart as I'll ever be.

Being like-minded when it came to work, Peggy was supportive in all the things that mattered to me. During our first years of marriage, if I had to work late I wouldn't get a nagging call to come home, like other guys I knew. She always gave me the freedom to work as hard as I wanted. She knew I needed to chase our dreams. Work was my medicine, my measuring stick, my life. It didn't take long for me to become a workaholic, and work became my god.

That led me to eventually invest our $25,000 we had saved into my first business, Eagle Vending. We were twenty-three years old at the time. Though it took me a year to finish the plans, I designed a bubble gum vending machine with two partners, Jay Ott and Harold Crandall. Soon we placed those little machines all over town, the kind where you put a quarter, turn the knob, and the gumball comes out.

Of course, this was more than just an evening hobby. I threw myself into my night work at Eagle Vending. It wasn't unusual for me to spend 80 to 100 hours a week working, between my full time design jobs at Xerox and Hughes Aircraft and my night job of Eagle Vending.

It didn't take long for me to figure out that this business venture wasn't rocket science, either. We were just making products that people needed. I also learned that business was also about keeping your word, improving existing products, and making things happen at a profit.

The vending company prospered. Actually, it grew like crazy, and pretty soon we were doing three or four million a year in sales. That's a lot of quarters, dimes and nickels. But despite all the hard work, and despite the early success, I remember feeling like we were still off the mark. I was a minority owner, anyway. Maybe I wasn't quite satisfied because I'd always been a bit of a perfectionist. Even my first success as an entrepreneur wasn't quite good enough.

So there I was, a few years into my new adventure ... and worrying about growing enough. I thought if I stayed with these two partners, stayed with this company, I would never reach my goals in time. Even though we were doing quite well, I knew I would never make a million by the time I was thirty. And if I couldn't accomplish my goal, I wouldn't be happy. I wouldn't feel fulfilled. I wouldn't realize the American Dream my parents brought me to this country to claim.

What could I do about it?

I really don't know how I had time to even worry. After all, I was still working for Xerox during the days as a design engineer. I would float back and forth between Xerox and Hughes, taking on more and more work, always wondering where I'd find something bigger or better. It was out there, somewhere. I just knew it had to be.

By this time I was completely living and breathing work. It had my full attention. I would obsess over making the right decisions and worry about potential problems. I kept telling myself, "Don't sit still. Don't be satisfied. And above all, don't stop."

I wish I had known Jesus at this time of my life. But instead of relying on the Lord, I relied even more on myself. In the process, work grew to become a curse, instead of the blessing God intends. Here's where it went really wrong. I thought if I could just work a little longer, push a little harder, I'd reach that pot at the end of the rainbow. But of course the desire was never satisfied, and the flame nearly consumed me.

Looking back, I realize how I was driven by fear—the fear of losing it all. The fear that whispered in my ear, saying…*Loser! This will never last. One day you'll wake up, and it'll all be gone, like a dream… poof! Fall asleep for a second and you'll be left with nothing. No wife. No friends. No money. No security. It happened to you once, you know. It can happen again.*

How could I argue? I listened to that fear every day, even though it would often get me down, hit me in the stomach and knock the wind out of me. The fear kept me running, scrambling to escape. The only way I could stay one step ahead was to reach for another new project, grab at a better job.

I've needed something to worry about in my entire life, in order to actually feel somewhat normal. At times I've actually made up problems in my mind. Crazy, huh?

Of course, I'd been running from this fear ever since I was a kid, back in Cuba. Back then the fear tackled me when our family lost everything overnight. It had chased us from a beautiful island to a run-down neighborhood in South Los Angeles. It chased me though my worst years of drugs and dumb mistakes. It continued to chase me, nipping at my heels and keeping me on edge.

Yet the fear helped me see something else, something new. I began to realize that I wanted...I *needed* to be my own boss. I didn't want to rely on someone else for a paycheck. I wanted to rely on myself. I also realized that if I was going to fulfill that dream of a being a millionaire by age thirty, I'd better get moving. I was already twenty-five, and I only had five years to go.

I would have to run even faster.

CHAPTER 8

DOGGING IT

"...we also rejoice in our sufferings, because we know that suffering produces perseverance; perseverance, character; and character, hope."
(Romans 5:3-4)

Baby and Story didn't know it at the time, but they had a lot to do with pushing me in a brand new direction. Of course, I'm talking about the family dogs, and they couldn't help that they were rough on their little wooden dog houses that I'd built them. Oh, and the weather, too. Between hairy dogs and winter rain, my home-made dog shelters were always falling apart.

It wasn't completely my fault, though. I knew how to swing a hammer. But even the guys in the TV handyman shows couldn't make a doghouse that would last forever. So one weekend I was grumbling to myself about the problem, asking myself...

Why can't somebody build a dog house that will stand up to abuse? And while we're at it, how about one that's easy to clean, too?

Why not? At this point an idea was forming in my head. Maybe I could create a better dog house, something completely different from the old plywood and two-by-four specials. After all, I knew a little bit about design. It couldn't be such a big leap.

So I started thinking about it from a business point of view. Maybe we could make this happen. Besides, by this time in my life I knew I needed to take control of my career, do something different. I was a little tired of slogging through one engineering assignment after another, day after day. My mind was going numb, really, and I didn't like the way I hated my life some days.

Besides, I knew things could change in a hurry and I could lose everything overnight, at any time. Life in Cuba taught me that. I knew I could be fired, or my programs downsized without notice. The company could be sold or reorganized. I didn't like how all those possibilities lay beyond my grasp, way outside my control.

Maybe that's why I'd always been so big into contingencies: planning ahead times two. I always thought about what could go wrong, always dug deep into the meanings behind every possible situation. I would try to figure things out, two or three steps ahead. What could happen next? And after that? And why?

At this point, that kind of planning ahead could often cross the line into compulsion. Contingencies are good, but not when you have contingencies for contingencies. My dad warned me that too much of a good thing was never good, and he was right. Ultimately my worry and my hyperagenda didn't leave room for God in my life. My compulsive contingencies robbed me of the simple joy of discovering God's hand in my life each day. I had no idea what it was like to trust God.

It would take a while for me to start to learn that trust lesson. I still struggle with it. Meanwhile, I began to look for new market opportunities. I wanted to escape the engineering dead end I thought I'd worked myself into. I wanted to find a Big Idea that would launch me to the front of the parade. Something fresh. Something that had never been done before. Something like the indestructible, easy-to-clean dog house.

The concept seemed promising, and I began working through the details. Of course, that was nothing new. I was constantly writing odd little notes, letters, and doodles of new brainstorms. But every other time, I would hesitate just long enough to watch some of my concepts make it to the market—thought of by someone else. I think Peggy was getting sick of hearing about all my big ideas that never quite made it.

"If you don't do this," she told me one day in the car, "someone else will. And you're going to regret it for the rest of your life."

That was all I needed to hear—all I needed to help push me from the dreaming stage to actual, serious design. I got together with my friend Darrell Paxman at Hughes Aircraft and together we designed a better dog house. Darrell was my boss at Hughes Aircraft who was also a brilliant engineer and an awesome family man. He and I went on to build a huge company.

Naturally we couldn't make it out of wood, like all my failed backyard efforts. We would use structural foam plastic—a material I knew well. After all, I'd designed covers for Xerox copy machines by using a new plastic molding process. We actually injected nitrogen gas into the plastic, which made the copiers much quieter because this enhanced plastic turned out to be a much better sound insulator. And what it did for sound, I thought, with a little modification maybe it would do for heat and cold, too. We would create a plastic dog house to keep pets warmer in the winter and cooler in the summer.

Great! We had the perfect material that would last forever and never rot, unlike wood. Our nitrogen-injected plastic would insulate better and clean up easily, just like I envisioned. We knew how to mass produce the material cheaply, with very little labor. But what about a design?

At first we thought a typical A-frame would serve. But even though you see that design a lot and it's been around a long time, we weren't satisfied with its built-in flaws—like excess space, difficult assembly and a high center of gravity. So, once more my wife came to the rescue with a better idea.

Over dinner one night I was talking to Peggy about the problems we'd run into with the design. After I'd explained everything she just looked over at me and dropped the answer in my lap.

"Be different," she told me. "You know, something unique. Why not make it an igloo shape? Will that work?" I told you she was smart.

Would it? At first I wasn't sure. But the more I thought about it, the more the igloo concept made sense. It had a lot of advantages over the traditional A-frame design, after all. So the next day Darrell and I jumped on the computer to design the ultimate dog house—in the shape of an igloo.

That turned out to be the easy part. Raising $80,000 to fabricate expensive new injection molds would be much tougher. But there was no way around it: We needed molds to mass produce the new dog houses. Oh, and add to that another $30,000 to make the first supply of dog houses for sale.

"Are you serious?" We got asked that a lot as we tried to find investors who would buy into the concept. "Why would anyone spend eighty grand to make dog houses?" Very strange-looking dog houses, for that matter. And I suppose it didn't help that Darrell and I were only in our twenties.

"It'll never work." We heard that a lot, too, if we got any response at all. And after a few turndowns we knew it was going to take a person with real vision to see beyond today and take a chance on tomorrow.

We finally did find that person in Stacy Tavis, the design engineer in charge of new products for a large custom structural foam molding company. After we explained it to him, Stacy not only believed in our idea, he also turned out to be a great cheerleader. Turns out that Stacy specialized in the kind of ideas that others would shy away from.

Of course, everyone else had turned down the idea for good reason. Because of its complicated shape and very large size, this was going to be one big engineering challenge. In fact, the igloo design threw us several curves we couldn't overcome—at first. Good thing Stacy looked past the obstacles and kept working with us.

But back to the start-up money. Despite Stacy's help, at first we had only enough cash to get our molds partially started. That didn't deter me though. I was determined for this to succeed, so for several months I worked 60-80 hour weeks at Xerox, saving the money we needed to complete the molds on time. Call me driven, determined… and worried.

By now my drive and my work habits fit the pattern: I lived to work; work had my complete attention. I obsessed about getting enough money to get started and worried about everything that might go wrong. Remember the compulsive contingencies? That meant I couldn't slow down, because we had so much riding on this venture. I pushed my nagging worries aside as much as I could and focused on my target of making this dog house venture fly.

After twelve intense months and a lot of encouragement from Stacy Tavis, we finally perfected the igloo-shaped plastic dome we would ultimately market as the "Dogloo." This was the summer of 1987, I had just turned twenty-seven years old, and we were ready for our public debut. So we decided to unveil the Dogloo at the Western World Pet Show in Long Beach. This would be our big break.

Wrong. Instead of compliments and orders we got laughs. An igloo-shaped dog house? What a scream. It turned out to be the show's big joke, and it turned my stomach to realize that the idea I'd been working so hard on and for so long, might've just crashed and burned. I went from great hope to great heartache, all in just a couple of days. I went home and broke down.

The hope had evaporated, I told Peggy. I'd lost our $60,000 and Darrell's $40,000 on a bad dream, and nobody was interested in our idea for a new dog house. The proof? Barely any interest shown and barely any orders taken. We did get one small order from Jim Daugherty, the founder of PetSmart. The (now huge) retail pet chain had two stores at the time. That was nice, but not exactly a return on the investment. I was sorely tempted to forget about the whole thing, but I just couldn't. I still nursed a tiny spark of hope.

Or maybe I was just stubborn. Either way, we figured this was time to move to phase two of the plan. We would take Dogloo to the streets, hand-sell them one by one, even if it meant discounting them to bargain-hunters at local swap meets on the weekends. I knew I would have to work really hard to persevere—and I was determined to succeed.

So the next day I took a sample Dogloo to "Pride and Groom," one of the most upscale pet stores in the Los Angeles area. I didn't feel much better when the owner, Larry Canter, took a look at my houses—and laughed.

"Who's going to buy a dog house that looks like an igloo?" he asked. "I wouldn't pay for something like that."

Well, maybe not. But that didn't stop me from bartering with Larry and giving him my best reasons why this design was so great. I had to get my dog houses into this store. I had to convince him. So even though he was still laughing, he finally agreed to take a few houses on consignment, and pay me only if they sold. Maybe he thought he was doing me a favor. Oh well. I did manage to slip in two conditions, though: One, he had to set them up in a prime location, near the store entrance. And two, he had to price them right.

So what happened? By the next week both Dogloos had sold, and Larry Cantor was amazed. So was I, for that matter. Even so, I still couldn't get advance payment for the next Dogloos at his store; he wasn't convinced they would keep selling. It was a fluke, maybe?

Well, that was okay. Because by that time I was starting to rediscover a little hope. And after a few months I was convinced that if the business was ever going to really break loose, it would need my full time attention. It would take a giant leap of faith.

I quit my job at Xerox.

It's not hard to guess what people thought of my decision. My old boss, Bill MacCleod, just shook his head. He had been such a great mentor through the years, and had taught me how to look at things creatively. Still he couldn't understand the logic behind this move.

And my parents? I figured they would see things my way—at first. Almost shaking with excitement, I pulled them into their living room one evening to explain everything and to show them how great this idea really was and where it would take us. Surely they would understand. But maybe they were expecting a different announcement. Because they just looked at me with a totally confused expression when I began to assemble a Dogloo right there in the middle of the floor. What was I doing?

I made my big announcement about leaving my safe, solid engineering career behind to pursue a fortune in dog houses. As I told them how big this would be, my parents just looked at me, then looked at each other. They didn't say a word.

Maybe they just needed a little more time to understand what this was all about. I could convince them. I broke the heavy silence by personally introducing them to our fabulous new product. Just as I had done back in Larry Cantor's pet shop, I explained the advantages and features of the best dog houses on the planet. Now they would get it.

Still no reaction.

"Can't you see this making millions, Dad?" I nearly shouted. Hey, I was pretty excited about this, after all.

I still remember the deer-in-the-headlights look on their faces as I tried my best to sell them on this new and improved idea. Their eyes were big as saucers, because they knew their son had gone over the edge. Looking back at it, I realized by this time they were probably in shock. For them this had turned into major trauma.

I wish I could have made the announcement differently. But years later I learned that I should not have been surprised; their reaction was actually very common. In fact, most people don't recognize new opportunities until they appear in the rear-view mirror. By then, of course, it's too late. The opportunity is gone.

And the same holds for deeper beliefs, because people tend to choose the *now* over *what could be*, the *obvious* instead of *what seems hidden*, the *safe* choice rather than the *risk*. We all have a tough time looking past the immediate, beyond what's happening right in front of us.

I understand all that now. But it still breaks my heart to see how people cling to their safety net of the present day. They lose their only opportunity to take hold of a future hope. Without hope of a promise, after all, there's no life and no future. That was true when I was introducing the Dogloo, and it's just as true today. It applies to the parts of life far beyond dog houses, too. After all, the Bible says that *"…hope that is seen is no hope at all. Who hopes for what he already has?"* (Romans 8:24)

Nobody. That's the whole point. What's more, we will never do the greatest things in life…until we first believe they can actually be done. And until we believe, we can't become the people God intends us to be.

So back then, nobody else believed in the Dogloo dream except Darrell and of course Peggy. Yes, Peggy believed in me, always had. Good thing, too. Because in the months ahead, I was definitely going to need her continued encouragement and support.

CHAPTER 9

FINDING THE AMERICAN DREAM

Yet when I surveyed all that my hands had done and what I had toiled
to achieve, everything was meaningless, a chasing after the wind;
nothing was gained under the sun... I hated all the things I had
toiled for under the sun, because I must leave them
to the one who comes after me.
(Ecclesiastes 2:11, 18)

That first year of business, 1987, we sold 1,800 Dogloos to local Southern California mom-and-pop pet stores. And yes, we had to work hard for each sale. Most of the store owners reacted the same way Larry Cantor had, that first day I'd tried to convince him to carry the new design. We got used to the laughs.

The really funny thing, though, was how differently pet owners reacted. Right from the start they loved the Dogloo—and so did their dogs. So even though we'd gotten off to a slow start, pretty soon word started getting around, and the houses started selling.

It wasn't until Sam Walton (of Walmart) picked up our Dogloos for Sam's Clubs that things started picking up. While I had never actually met Sam Walton, I had read his books about Walmart and the American dream. Sam Walton had become an American hero to me. So it was surreal when on my thirty-second birthday, Peggy had surprised me with a personal letter from Sam Walton congratulating me and personally thanking me for our contributions to the success of Walmart stores. Imagine that, a personal letter from my hero! It was the real deal. Peggy beamed with pride as she handed me the letter that she had framed. To me, the letter from Sam Walton was as American as apple pie. It was Walmart who made Dogloo an American icon.

Anyway, back to business. Our second year, we sold 18,000 units—enough to make us start to think that we might have a hit on our hands, after all. After Sam's Club and Walmart picked up Dogloos, we started selling over 100,000 Dogloos in the third year. Had we started the newest revolution in pet housing? As we dared to ask the question, Darrell handled operations, while I was in charge of sales and marketing. Together we watched the money pour in, faster and faster, even beyond what we could have hoped for.

In fact, we made millions in the early years. Around 1993, outside appraisers valued Dogloo Inc. at over $40 million, just five years after our annual earnings pushed past the $4 million mark. It didn't stop there, either. By 1997, Dogloo Inc. had leapfrogged to $62 million in yearly sales, and $8 million in earnings.

Sixty-two million! Who would have thought? Just ten years after I'd made that bumbling announcement to my parents, I was the chief executive officer of a company with a staff of more than 600 employees. We operated two factories in the U.S. and sold Dogloos in over 42 countries.

Wasn't this exactly what I'd dreamed about for so long? The rags-to-riches story, the immigrant who struck gold? Before we knew it, Darrell and I would call ourselves millionaires many times over. We had achieved the American dream!

But fasten your seatbelts—we still had a way to go. From the original Dogloo design we added dozens of items to our catalog until we were producing and marketing 200 different products, with distribution worldwide. Now customers could buy Dogloos for any sized dog, from Chihuahua to Great Dane—with special accessories like sleeping pads or protective flaps for the opening.

With all these products, though, the game got complicated in a hurry. We quickly outgrew the companies that supplied us with raw materials and custom products, and in 1995 we broke ground in Indianapolis on a new $20 million state-of-the-art manufacturing plant. How else could we keep up with skyrocketing customer orders? This is when I started to believe I wasn't bulletproof, because we began to trip over our own feet.

And this is where I should have listened to sound business

advice, because this kind of growth turned out to be too much, too quick. Practically overnight, we went from a sales and marketing focused company to a state-of-the-art manufacturing company, and understandably our staff was unprepared for the leap. I don't fault them for this. Among other things, we miscalculated the time required to get the new plant operating. So we slipped from making over $4 million in profits before opening the plant, to losing $2.5 million the very next year of operating the new plant. The bottom line: my pride, greed and ego had driven us to expand too quickly.

Even so, I have to admit I was a bit shocked when Darrell pulled me aside one day, not long after we got the new plant on line.

"Sit down," he told me. "We need to talk." His eyes told me this was no joke. "We're millions in debt."

As it turned out, by that time we were about $40 million in debt and that wasn't exactly pocket change. In fact, such an extreme debt load was more than enough to drag our success train to a quick and screeching halt. So when Bank of America called our loans, I was forced to scramble, bringing in outside money and investors to keep the banks happy. I had no choice, really. What else could I have done? But I knew it was only a Band-Aid on a deep wound. Darrell and I could only watch helplessly as controlling interest of the company slipped through our fingers. We both knew this was the beginning of the end.

I distinctly remember how I cried at home after my kids had gone to sleep, not long after the mess with the banks. Peggy and I called out to God for forgiveness and for His help. And make no mistake, God did help us, in His sovereign way. We would see that in the months to come, even if we didn't recognize His hand at first.

Meanwhile, I had no time to catch my breath as I worked feverishly with the investors to rescue the company from that scary losing year. We had to yank it back over to profitability once again, and fast.

Or else.

So we ramped up to run the new manufacturing plant 24/7, put our shoulders behind the business, and pushed. And the very next year after that embarrassing loss we turned a $6.7 million profit. That was the good news. The bad news was that it was still too late for Darrell and me; Dogloo was no longer our company. Almost overnight, the fun, creative atmosphere from years before just melted away as we were converted into a corporate moneymaking machine. Now we belonged to an out-of-town group of shrewd investors.

As for me, I'd learned my lesson...too late. Yes, I still had a job, and I still reported for duty for the next two years. I still worked hard and I still kept the company moving ahead. Partly that was because it was hard to step away; I was so plugged into the everyday routine of the company. And another part was because I was committed to all the good people who had worked so hard for me in the past. But I came to genuinely hate my job and nearly everything about it. I couldn't keep this up.

Finally on the morning of my thirty-seventh birthday, my life melted down. Here it was my tenth anniversary at Dogloo, and I awoke with a horribly fresh sense of dread as I faced the maze of meaningless commitments I knew the day would hold. Why even get up? Everything seemed so horribly futile as I hid under the covers. Was I doing anything that mattered, really? Did I make a difference, or was I just a puppet for the new investors?

Perhaps I'd felt my strings yanked one time too many. After we brought in the investors I reported to three people, three bosses. The stress ratcheted up as I did my best to keep the new board of directors happy. But all the time spent dealing with things like ownership issues and debt restructuring distracted me from the real business of building a future for the company. Sometimes the smoke from those brush fires chased us in directions I knew weren't best for Dogloo, Inc.

Sure, we would top $62 million in sales that year, and over $8 million in profits. And sure, I learned a lot while working for the new investors. They taught me much about business and finance.

Maybe too much.

Prime Example: That year I had been working to acquire our competitor, a larger company out of Texas. I was prepared to make a deal work, only not the way it turned out. Because once the new investor group was convinced, they pushed hard to acquire the competition—at whatever the cost. And though I could see how the steep price for this company could quickly grow into a problem, I was powerless to stop what was happening. It was like a huge freeway pileup coming at me, only in slow motion. And soon it led the investors to make drastic decisions.

First, both of our Dogloo manufacturing facilities would be consolidated into one. I could deal with that. But I could not deal with the other part of that decision: My entire staff was to be terminated, fired, laid off. Just like that.

Well, not the entire staff. About ninety-five percent were let go. As if these hard-working people had no value. This directive devastated me, dragging me into a dark period in my life. Even after

I had reluctantly climbed out of bed that gloomy birthday morning, the last thing I wanted was to be the hatchet man. And maybe this pushed me over the edge. Because I knew then that Darrell and I had to get out quickly, before it was too late.

So we decided, and a few months later I negotiated to sell our interest in Dogloo. Though we were forced to leave literally millions on the table, when I finally made it out I'd gathered over $21 million in the last ten years. Of course, that was before taxes, so much of it went to the government.

Well, that sounds pretty good to most people. Most people would have expected me to be ecstatic about this kind of deal. Instead I was paralyzed by the thought of losing our company. Suddenly I realized that for me, Dogloo had served as the rock of my life, one huge constant, a place to hang my coat—and my instability. I had counted on this dream for the past ten years. Now, for me, Darrell and our families, Dogloo was dead. The company we had sacrificed for and built, was gone forever—a chasing after the wind.

As it turned out, the new merged company ran into severe financial difficulties three years after Darrell and I left—even though both companies made a lot of money before the merger, and even though they wrapped up an eighty percent of market share after the deal. Apparently the new management and board made some poor strategic decisions. So looking back, leaving the company at that time turned out to be a blessing—even though we didn't get as much money out of the deal as we had hoped for. At least Darrell and I got out safely. God surely had a better plan for us.

Only, what was it, exactly? Call me clueless. My friends and family called me a royal success. Everywhere I went, people congratulated me, the way they would congratulate a person who had just won the lottery. And of course I kept up appearances, the success façade. So people kept cheering me on, with high five after high five.

I had crossed the finish line. Yet oddly enough, the more I was congratulated, the more depressed I grew. The more people told me "Way to Go!" the more I doubted, the more I felt like a failure, the more I knew I'd made huge mistakes. And as the months flew by, I began to ask myself darker and darker questions. What was significant? What did it all mean?

CHAPTER 10

CROSSING THE FINISH LINE

What more can the king's successor do than what has already been done?... So I hated life, because the work that is done under the sun was grievous to me. All of it is meaningless, a chasing after the wind.
(Ecclesiastes 2:12b,17)

Everything changed after Darrell and I sold our shares in Dogloo. Never mind the money. Without a job to report to every day, I had a little more time to think. And that was dangerous.

I kept wondering why nothing ever seemed to add up. Why was I no happier now than before I'd graduated to the millionaire club? Even more than that, I started wondering what would happen to me if I were to die, and I wondered why I was even born. What was the point?

Of course I had no answers, not even a hint, so now I was more lost than ever. So like ants discovering sugar, the old insecurities quickly crept back into my wounded life, and started carrying off the pieces.

And the difference now was painfully obvious: I no longer owned an escape route. Before, I had tried to mask my emptiness and insecurities with work. Now I didn't even have that crutch. I couldn't throw myself into my job, the place where I used to hide and ignore the feelings. I'd lost my only identity. The business, the job, the work was gone—leaving me with... what, exactly?

I sure didn't know that, either. And with nothing to hold back the tide, these insecurities and their accompanying pain continued to grow. The only thing I could think of doing was to go ahead and live life big, dive head first and all the way into the full material scene. We went on a bit of a spending spree. We always traveled first class. We vacationed all over the world, meeting famous and powerful people.

And once again the words of King Solomon echoed loudly in my life: *"This too is meaningless, a chasing after the wind."* (Ecclesiastes 2:26b) Where had I heard that before?

Here's another example of what I was thinking at the time. Not long before we sold the company, I'd bought a Porsche turbo—one of those amazing sports cars with an amazing price tag (about $150,000). World class, eh? Well, it had always been one of my goals to own one, so I figured I should go ahead and have it. More than nearly anything else I could own, this car would announce to the world that I had arrived. Success! That's what I thought it would say—and loudly. I wasn't prepared for what really happened, though.

Oh, I was plenty excited to get in and drive it for the first time. I was eager to turn the key and hear the throaty roar as I pulled away from the dealership. *Check out this piece of German engineering*, I thought. But I was shocked to feel that new car buzz fade more quickly than I'd ever dreamed—and there was nothing I could do to hold on to it. And this is the truth: Before I'd even made it home that first time, the car had already lost its appeal.

"Is this it?" I asked myself. As if I'd unwrapped a birthday present, but the box was empty. I was as puzzled as anyone by what had happened, though of course I couldn't let on. "Come on. Is this really all there is?"

I got no answers. Still I kept asking that question in the months after we sold our interest in Dogloo. And soon I bottomed out emotionally and spiritually. Here I was, thirty-seven years old and just three months into my golden retirement, and we decided to take off on a vacation with my beautiful wife and three wonderful kids to an unspoiled area of New Zealand. On the surface, nothing could be better. What a cool adventure, after all, and what a beautiful place.

Yet even in that amazing place, my depression gripped me, shook me, and would not let go.

In my head I knew I should have been happy, content, and fulfilled. Yet everything I did on that vacation only came back to slap me in the face—a cruel reminder that the rest of my life was as hollow as the thrill I'd found driving my new Porsche home. Some thrill. Some life. And there in the middle of all that incredible scenery it became harder and harder to keep a smile on my face as I fell headfirst into a deep, black hole of depression.

Once more, for probably the third time ever, I was almost ready to just check out of life. I kept thinking, *"If this is all that this world has to offer, then I'm done. There's just no purpose. Even if I could make another million bucks, why would I? For what?"*

As I asked myself these questions, the thrill of the world-class vacation turned sour. I got tired of those great five-star dinners, I got tired of the beautiful beaches. I got tired of packing and unpacking. Just like I'd already tired of the fancy cars, the accomplishments, the perks. By this point I got tired of… well, pretty much everything—because one thing was true:

It was all just *stuff.*

Stuff and more stuff, cluttering up my empty life. I had reached a point where I knew the rest of the act didn't matter, anymore. The haunting insecurity that had chased me all my life had finally caught up once more, tagging me halfway across the world. And when it did, it bowled me over.

So was anyone keeping score? The drugs hadn't filled the void, when I was younger. Strike one. Neither had the trophy girlfriends. Strike two. Now the money and the success I'd desperately wanted for so long couldn't help me, either. The only thing they filled was my bank account. And I didn't care about that, because my heart and soul were still empty. As empty as ever.

Strike three.

So as I toured New Zealand's gorgeous mountains and fjords, I had a pretty good idea that I had taken a very wrong turn somewhere. Not in New Zealand, but in life. By that time I could clearly tell that I was dragging around nothing more than dead man's bones. And whether I knew it yet or not, whether I wanted to admit it, this hard-working, responsible, moral man was headed for hell. The worst part was I had no clue how to fix my problem.

So what else could I do but pack up my bags (again!), and head back home with my family, all the while keeping that fake smile on my face. Only Peggy knew the pain and despair I was in.

On the plane my mind raced, trying to sort through my options. Okay, so what was wrong with this picture, really? I'd finally made it financially into the fast lane, but not the way I'd wanted to. I was lost and yet looking for answers. Wasn't there some way all of this could bring me closer to God, or at least somewhere close to His neighborhood?

Not likely. I would pray every night, even though God didn't seem to answer back. I strained my ears to hear a shred of wisdom, some kind of sign. Anything. Yet God remained silent.

Sometimes I felt like screaming a protest at the Almighty, maybe like King David in the Old Testament. In fact, the first three verses of Psalm 13 could have been my theme song back then, if I'd known it:

"How long, O LORD? Will you forget me forever? How long will you

hide your face from me? How long must I wrestle with my thoughts and every day have sorrow in my heart? How long will my enemy triumph over me? Look on me and answer, O LORD my God. Give light to my eyes, or I will sleep in death..."

That's the way I felt, too. But still God didn't seem to answer my call. All I could do was shake my head and wonder what was wrong.

I found out later that God really did feel my deepest pain. He was actually there all the time, only it was not time—yet. He was hard at work in my life, breaking me, helping me to understand how nothing in this world could ever make me happy or fill my emptiness. Back then, though, I was just looking for a break. How much deeper would I have to sink before I began to see things His way?

Just a little bit deeper, I found out soon enough. Because once I sold the company, I started to experience more and more anxiety attacks. The depression of my youth was back upon me. Shortly after we returned from New Zealand, I started feeling sharp chest pains while attending a meeting at Young President's Organization, a group of young entrepreneurs. No joke. Suddenly I couldn't catch my breath, and I panicked. This couldn't be happening to me!

They rushed me to the emergency room, and I figured I had a pretty good idea of what had happened. I'd seen all the doctor shows on TV. I knew what heart attacks were supposed to be like. And after hours of extensive examinations, my friend John Calderon, the president of the hospital, came to me with terrible news. The worst I could imagine.

"I am afraid there is nothing physically wrong with you," he told me.

What? If I'd really suffered a heart attack, the doctors could have given me a prescription. They would have pointed to the x-rays, written out a plan of action, given me some hope. We could have solved this "why" problem the way a good engineer would.

But this? How was I supposed to fight an enemy I couldn't see? All I knew was that this was the same phantom that had chased me here from Cuba and all the way to Los Angeles, in and out of trouble, now halfway across the world and back. The same nameless fears I'd known when I woke up and couldn't make myself go to work. That same black cloud that had hovered over Darrell and me when we lost Dogloo to the investors. Yes, that was the one.

And what pained me now was nothing the doctor could recognize, let alone cure. To discover my cure I had to take a different path, a new direction.

I needed to go on a journey of faith.

CHAPTER 11

CALLED TO THE PRINCIPAL'S OFFICE

For God so loved the world that he gave his one and only Son, that whoever believes in him shall not perish but have eternal life. For God did not send his Son into the world to condemn the world, but to save the world through him. Whoever believes in him is not condemned, but whoever does not believe stands condemned already because he has not believed in the name of God's one and only Son.
(John 3:16-18)

For a while nothing changed. I had survived the New Zealand vacation (barely) and we'd made it back to our nice "little" 15,000-square-foot house with the swimming pool and the two housekeepers. There's no place like home, right? But I was still searching, begging God for something to lift me out of my personal black hole, the depression that sucked the life out of me every day.

At least I still had three great kids and a wonderful wife, but I knew they deserved more than a hollow mannequin for a dad and a husband. I was certain of that much. For my part, well, I wasn't quite sure what I deserved, actually. I hoped it was more than a crippled lifetime of doubts, questions and anxieties.

The confusing part was, I thought I had tried everything to put my life on track—including religion. After all, I would pray every night. I was a moral guy. Hey, I donated expensive computers to my kids' Christian school. I even publicly gave God the credit for the whole Dogloo success story…more than once.

So what was the problem? Why wasn't I connecting with God— or why wasn't He connecting with me? And why was my life still such a mess? I still didn't get it.

That's why I will never forget Wednesday afternoon, March 18, 1998. I was working through some of the details of that computer donation during a visit to my children's school, Woodcrest Christian, in Riverside. As I chatted with the School Superintendent there, Randy Thompson, he mentioned what my daughter CoLene had written in her diary which was part of a school assignment.

I wondered if something was wrong. No. In fact, Randy told me how impressed he was by what she'd written. He called it a great testimony.

Well, that was fine, I thought. But I wondered out loud how a sixth grade girl could possibly truly know God. And that's probably what tipped him off.

Randy didn't comment on what I'd said, but simply invited me to lunch. Sure, I was up for that. We found a restaurant where we talked business and a few other issues. And then Randy got ready to drop the bomb.

"Hey Aurelio," he said, with that friendly smile of his. "I really want to thank you so much. You're always here for us, whatever we need…"

"You're welcome, Randy." Sure thing. I was getting used to telling people "you're welcome." That was part of being a Big Donor. But then he looked me straight in the eye, and totally changed the direction of the conversation.

"You know, Aurelio, you're a nice guy, and (on the outside) you look really good and all, but…"

Where was he going with this?

"But it seems as if there's something missing in your life," he said. "Is there? What are you looking for?"

By this time I was just about falling over in my chair. Something missing? I hadn't told him what really happened during our vacation in New Zealand. I hadn't shared anything personal with him, like the dark underbelly of my life story. No way. Nothing like that. And now he was doing this mind-reading routine?

I think I finally managed to croak out something like, "What do you mean?"

He said, "I get the feeling there's something that isn't right."

Well, this hit me between the eyes, obviously. But for some reason I didn't squirm away. For some reason I actually answered him—honestly.

"I guess I'm tired, Randy. Sometimes I just want to get off the treadmill. I want wisdom, purpose and peace in my life."

True, so far. But then he asked me something like whether I knew for certain that if I were to die tonight, would I go to heaven.

Oh, wow. I decided I might as well lay everything on the table.

"To tell the truth, Randy." I may have paused right then, but out it came. "I'm scared to death that if I die, I'll go to hell."

What was he going to say to that? Here was the principal of a Christian school, after all. I didn't know if I should duck—or run. But he nodded as if he knew just what I was saying.

"You know, I was there one time."

"Really? What did you do?"

"I met a man who helped me."

Well, this was sounding more and more suspicious, but still I listened. And Randy told me that if I followed him back to his office, he would introduce me to this man.
Uh-oh. What was this, some kind of motivational speaker?

Because if it was, I'd heard it all. By now I really wasn't so sure about all this.

But I was polite and this was my kid's principal, so I followed him. I figured I didn't have anywhere else to go at the time.

But I wasn't totally naïve. I knew who this man was, and I basically knew what he stood for. So in the back of my mind I started hoping desperately that he wasn't going to talk to me about God.

Please, anything but that. Even a motivational speaker would have been better, I thought.

So we got to his office and he closed the door. What kinds of conversations took place behind a closed door at the principal's office? Doors closed before people got fired, or reprimanded. I knew all about that. This was turning serious, all of a sudden. Now I was sweating.

First thing I did was glance around, and there it was. The Bible on the table. And I thought, *I knew it! A set up! An ambush!*

Why couldn't he have just told me in advance, so I could have planned something in my schedule that would have conflicted, so I could have told him, "Sorry, gotta go."

But now I was stuck. He knew it and I knew it. He told me to sit down, so I sat down. I could get through this. And then he started asking me questions. Questions like…

"Do you know Jesus?"

Oh. That one was easy.

"Of course I know Jesus," I answered back. Like, who doesn't? "He's the Son of God."

But Randy wasn't giving up that easily. Now he wanted to know what else I knew about the man.

"Well," I answered, "He was born at Christmas, and He rose from the grave at Easter. Right?"

Cute. But from that point Randy's questions got harder and more awkward. Some of them dug way deeper than I liked. This was getting personal. Still feeling ambushed, I squirmed in my chair and looked for a way out, an exemption, some excuse. Didn't it count that I was a successful businessman, a nice family man, a totally responsible, moral guy who donated to charities?

By this time I understood that Randy didn't care about any of those outside things. Instead he asked me about the things inside my life that I tried to sweep under the rug. He asked if I'd ever turned away from my sins. Uh. . .

Well, had I?

I knew I had plenty to hide. The pride over my accomplishments, the greed for more, jealousy…I could go on. Oh yes, I could go on.

So could Randy, and each question drilled me deeper and deeper. Like, did I know what the Bible said about those who have sinned, and how we've all sinned? Did I know the penalty for our sins on judgment day is hell, eternal separation from God? Did I believe there really is a place called hell, reserved for people who have sinned? The way it said in the Bible?

Uh…

And what about Jesus? He sprinkled in more Bible verses that explained how this Jesus paid the price for our sins on the cross, how Jesus is the solution to our sin problem. Randy got my attention, and obviously no one had ever talked to me like this before. No one had ever shared this mystery of Jesus with me. No one!

Could I believe in this truth, instead of believing in myself, instead of believing in the things of this world? How about all the good things I had done? I thought I'd done more good than bad. Couldn't I get into heaven riding on my good works, without Jesus?

By this time my doubts stared me in the face, but they looked pretty lame compared to the power of what Randy was explaining to me. Hey, the truth hurt. Speaking of power, though, something else was going on in my soul, something very real, like a strong ocean tide. My heart raced, convicted, like God was speaking straight to me.

I didn't know exactly what it was at the time, but later I would understand that the Holy Spirit of God was calling me—tugging at my soul. And He knew exactly where the handles were, even though they'd been buried deep all my life. But just like that, I was exposed and vulnerable, like I had nowhere left to hide.

Funny thing was, I knew then that I wanted this. I wanted to be saved; wanted my sins to be forgiven. How could I not? For the first time in my life—Click!—the light went on. God's light, not mine. By that light I could finally see what I'd been searching for all my life. There in Randy's office I finally realized what kind of gift Jesus wanted to give me, how much it had cost Him, and why I needed to stretch out my hand and say…

Yes.

Yes to His sacrifice on the cross for my sins—past, present and future. That day I realized Jesus loved me more than anyone else ever could. It was so hard to imagine, but so true. Jesus had a way of stepping through time. I broke down and started to sob.

Yes to the God who had followed me all the way from Cuba, waiting for me to shut up and listen. Yes to Jesus.

Yes, by this time I knew what kind of a deal was on the table. Jesus knew of every heartache and struggle in my past. He'd paid my enormous debt of the sins I had piled up over the years. And now He was ready to give me the kind of pardon I couldn't refuse. But I still had one question…

"Why would He do it?" I choked out the words. The offer seemed almost too good, too one-sided. Maybe there was some kind of catch. What kind of love was this, really?

So there I was sitting in an office across from Principal Thompson with my head in my hands, sobbing, a grown man at his lowest point ever. Lower than my teen screw-up years, lower than my depressions, lower even than when we were in New Zealand.

But this time was different, way different. This time I knew that when I reached out I would be given the most incredible gift ever: God's mercy, the grace of Jesus, everything that I had never deserved.

Right then, right there, I knew I had to choose Jesus over the things of this world, and call Him my Lord and my Savior. Forget waiting. I reached out to Jesus.

I felt like the thief on the cross who asked Jesus to remember Him in heaven. The thief on the cross who was being crucified beside Jesus asked Jesus not to forget Him when he died. Jesus looked at the thief and said "today you will be in paradise," all because the thief believed. Is this the most beautiful thing ever? This thief had no time to do anything good, he had no time to be baptized, he just came as he was and believed in Jesus Christ as his Lord and his Savior. And he was saved!

I was no different. And this! This offer of salvation was everything that I had been searching and longing for. The mystery of God! What I couldn't figure out was, how could I not have known earlier? For thirty-eight years, I had never heard the good news about Jesus, the solution to my sin nature. At least not like this. No one had ever taken the time to sit me down and really share the only truth that could change my life, until that day with Randy. Imagine that—a lifetime of stumbling along in the darkness, stubbing my toes, falling on my face without any hope or promise. You'd think I would have gotten a clue already.

I guess I'd just always assumed God operated on the same business model as me. If you want something, you work hard for it. I remember hearing "God helps those that help themselves," only to find out that it's not in the Bible and it couldn't be further from the truth.

I always thought a person could earn everything, work hard and attain salvation, right? If something's missing, you go out and hunt it down. But you always keep your hand on the wheel, and you always stay in control. I was pretty good at that, at the human traditions and basic principles of this world.

Now Jesus was turning everything upside-down. Everything I'd ever thought about God, well, I was dead wrong. To my surprise, I realized this was all about grace, and grace alone. So I came to Him full of pain and fear, grief and confusion, and He promised to take me in, His lost son, just like that.

I didn't deserve it and I hadn't earned it. But this was grace, after all—receiving what I didn't earn. That day I realized that as sinful as I was, and as dirty as I was, that through Jesus my sins would be forgiven. He would wash me clean. The only condition?

Accept. Give up. Surrender. Let go. Believe!

So that's what I did. I poured out my heart to God. I told Him what I'd done wrong—the jealousy, the ego, the pride, the doubts, the worries, the fears, the mistakes... all the rest. As if He didn't already know! And I surrendered control of my life over to Him that afternoon. One hundred percent. Permanently. Just like it says in the Bible, *"That if you confess with your mouth, 'Jesus is Lord,' and believe in your heart that God raised him from the dead, you will be saved. For it is with your heart that you believe and are justified, and it is with your mouth that you confess and are saved."* (Romans 10:9-10)

It's true: God heard my weeping, stooped down right next to me, and that day I was given a whole new life. A love I never knew before. Finally, the weight of carrying all the guilt and responsibility for so long was lifted. My life search ended at the beginning of a brand-new journey, right there in the principal's office. Just imagine! I walked into the principal's office spiritually dead, but stepped out into the hallway totally alive... alive in Jesus!

This was just the beginning of a work in progress, though. Because that same Holy Spirit who had been tugging on my soul now swept into my life and started rearranging all the furniture. Actually, it was more like a garage sale than a cleaning. Whatever it was, this process would turn out to be painful at times, too. Sometimes even more painful than I expected.

CHAPTER 12

INTO THE LIGHT

But as for you, continue in what you have learned and have become
convinced of, because you know those from whom you learned it,
and how from infancy you have known the holy Scriptures, which
are able to make you wise for salvation through faith in Christ Jesus.
All Scripture is God-breathed and is useful for teaching, rebuking,
correcting and training in righteousness, so that the man of
God may be thoroughly equipped for every good work.
(2 Timothy 3:14-17)

A week later Randy, the school principal, called me on the phone.

"Aurelio, we're starting a Bible study. I want you to come to it."

Just like that. Well, it shouldn't have surprised me, but at first I was a little confused. I didn't think I'd signed up for anything but an entry pass to heaven.

"What are you talking about?" I asked him. "I thought I was a Christian, now. You know, I'm done. Right?"

As in, I'd crossed the finish line, already. Honestly, that was my first impression of what had happened to me. But Randy didn't see it that way.

"No, Aurelio. If you don't go to church, if you don't feed on the Word, you're never going to grow."

Feed on the Word? Was that anything like eating a bowl of soup?

"But I'm saved, right?"

"Sure," he told me, "you're going to get into heaven. But your trials are going to come. Those aren't going to go away. How are you going to get through trials, without reading the Word?"

Well, I didn't have a good answer for him. So I went to his Bible study early the next Wednesday morning, kicking and screaming at first. But pretty soon I settled down. Turns out it was a good group of guys, all businessmen who really wanted to dig into the Bible and learn what God had for them. In addition to me, Randy would disciple Mike Van Daele, Scott Alden, Gordon Bourns and Greg Lane; all people who supported and encouraged me early on in my walk with God. What a concept!

I also found out in the weeks to come (yes, I went back) that the group was a good way for the men to keep tabs on each other. Hold each other accountable. So if we knew one of us had a big decision to make, we could pray for each other. Or if we were struggling with an issue, we didn't have to struggle alone. We could ask each other, "How's it going?" And not just get a fake answer.

Most of all, though, going to a weekly Bible study turned out to be like joining a gym, a place where I could build up my spiritual muscles. And since I had a lot to learn, I kept going to the study, week after week. I began really listening to the words in the Bible, doing what God told me to do. Sometimes it was hard, and sometimes I began to understand what Randy had told me about trials. I wasn't immune to trouble, just because I was a Christian, now. But I began learning as much of the Bible as I could. After I got over that first confusion, I couldn't get enough of God.

Yeah, I soaked it up. But sponges that just stay wet, get sour. I needed an outlet. So even while I was going to Bible studies I began praying that God would use whatever gifts and talents He had given me, for His glory. In other words, the spotlight was shifting away from Aurelio and straight towards the Lord; this was not all about me, anymore.

And what a relief that was! Once I realized what God had done for me, I wanted to share the news with everyone I met. Why not? After all, there had to be tons of people out there who were living life just the way I had lived it, totally in the dark, clueless.

That desire would lead to the rest of the story, and it would soon take me on an adventure I could never have imagined. But even as

God was preparing the way, I kept studying.

I began to learn of God's grace, about the fact that we are all sinners, but through the grace of Jesus not only are we saved, but it is also how we grow. We grow in grace, not by works so no man can boast. (Ephesians 2:8-9)

One of the first workbooks I tackled was called *Fundamentals of the Faith,* by John MacArthur. Chapter by chapter, I picked up an overview of the Bible, along with the differences between the Old Testament (the law) and the New Testament (grace). I learned what each of the sixty-six books in the Bible meant, why they were written, and how perfectly they meshed—even though they'd been penned by 42 different people over a period of thousands of years.

Of course God was behind it all. That's why it's funny to me how the media and secular authors will take shots at the Bible from time to time; trying to claim it contains contradictions or fairy tales. Each time, of course, the claims are proven bogus and God's Word stands. How could they understand the Bible, anyway?

To really understand the Bible, we need to meet at least two conditions. First, we have to be born again. We need to be saved by Jesus, and by our faith in Jesus we are saved. That's a basic; we're born again when we follow Jesus Christ in saving faith and take that definite step to commit all our ways to Him. Such a faith opens the door for the Holy Spirit to actually make a home in our soul, and in the process our eyes are opened to recognize differences between truth and fiction. That's called discernment.

God the Holy Spirit guides believers who are submitted to Him. If we're not, He won't. It's that simple. It is impossible to understand the Bible without the Holy Spirit dwelling in you, and He can only dwell in you through faith placed in Jesus.

The other condition for understanding the Bible is simply time. It's a big, deep book, and we need time to study. Years, I suppose. But if we're born again and we commit the time it takes to soak up the truth of God's Word, little by little, then we're finally qualified to offer intelligent interpretation. Otherwise...

Here's a good comparison: Imagine traveling to Russia, not knowing a word of Russian—and yet daring to offer detailed opinions about Russian literature. Sure, the Russians would take you seriously, right? They shouldn't. Yet those who don't know the Bible (or its Author) are quick to offer their opinions about how it was written or what it means. Right?

So back to my Bible studies. Some time after my first attempts to open the Bible with other believers, we went through the well-known twelve-week study called *Experiencing God,* by Henry Blackaby. Wow—this book changed my life. In very practical ways it showed me how to have an even more personal and meaningful relationship with God, how to fully experience Him in daily life. I believe that God Himself has used this book to turn on spiritual floodlights—and not just for me. But *Experiencing God* helped me learn more about what God is really like, how to hear His voice and then how to join Him where He is already working. This book challenged me in such a way that I knew I couldn't keep running away from Him.

What a change. As I went through this study, I noticed that God was becoming my trustworthy friend. Not a distant, unreachable God like before, but actually my personal mentor and teacher. I've gone through this book three times now because it's so rich and full of good advice.

Another book I read often is a daily devotional by Oswald Chambers called *My Utmost for His Highest.* Here's a Christian classic that has ministered to me greatly and brought me so much comfort and joy over the years. Maybe that's partly because of the way it's written, in a one-page-per-day format. It seems that every time I read a page it's as if God speaks to me and challenges me. *My Utmost* is also super practical and shows me how to plug God's Word into my life.

But wait, there's more: Another weekly Bible study that has helped me grow spiritually is Bible Study Fellowship International. BSF is a non-denominational, international Bible study organization that has women's and men's groups meeting weekly in cities all over the world. Studies start with a lecture and then break into smaller groups for us to go over the text. It's a must for me, and I believe God has given me favor for making his Word a priority and allowing me to faithfully attend my BSF men's study every week.

I do know from experience, however, that reading the Bible can be intimidating at first. And it can be tough without an experienced guide to help. So it's essential to join a Bible study group, where others can help you grow. We all need somebody to guide us and keep us accountable, whether it's a pastor, church elder, youth leader, or maybe just an experienced friend. Someone who understands God's Word and who cares enough to follow up on what we're learning. This kind of group shouldn't be too hard to find, either. Every Bible teaching church usually has a weekly Bible study that's perfect for different kinds of people.

Where to start? I think the best place for new believers to begin studying the Bible is in the New Testament, with the Gospel of John. This is the fourth gospel account, actually, after those written by Matthew, Mark and Luke. Of course, any of these books make a good place to dive into the Bible, but John takes special care to explain the meaning behind the life of Jesus. This is the book that opens with, *"In the beginning was the Word, and the Word was with God, and the Word was God."* (John 1:1) How about that!

Then in the Old Testament, Genesis would be my second choice of books to read. It's not hard to find, since it's the first book of the entire Bible. Before opening the Bible up to study, however, why not talk first with the author? I pray and ask God to teach me, to speak to me through His Word before I actually begin digging into the Bible. It has always helped and blessed me.

Listening to good preaching has also helped me understand God's Word, and it's a big part of my spiritual growth. I started the habit of listening to sermons on the radio while driving from place to place. I was shocked at how much I learned during drive-time. Some of my favorites: Charles Morris, Charles Stanley, John MacArthur, Chuck Swindoll, Alistair Begg, Greg Laurie… just to name a few.

Often as I've listened to Bible teaching on the radio, the Holy Spirit has touched my heart and shown me more about Himself— things I really ought to know. And as God convicted me of sin, I've surrendered to His will and wept with joy. Why did I carry those dead weights around for so long, when God wanted to take them from me? Looking back, it seems so obvious. And it's a blessing to know the ever-patient God who's willing to work with us and to teach us. But we do need to stop and listen. And eventually we can't avoid the very personal question:

What about you?

That's the question I had to answer for myself. No one else could answer it for me. What about you? You may be a millionaire, or you may struggle to pay the bills. You may be a model citizen, a big failure, or somewhere in between. You may love your family and even pray every night, attend church regularly, the way you think you're supposed to. Or maybe not.

But it all adds up to a big fat zero unless we believe, turn from our sin and make that commitment to follow Jesus. Sounds like a spiritual do-it-yourself project? Trust me, it doesn't work that way. I was following my own blueprint until I came face-to-face with my failure and realized that I am under God's grace. By His grace, I accepted Jesus Christ as Lord and Savior of my life. And if I (a prideful, ego driven man) did, so can anybody else (no matter what sin they're dealing with).

I do wish someone would have explained the truth about Jesus to me, much earlier in my life. But obviously I can't change that. And here's what changed my life so radically that day in Randy's office:

Realizing—I was a sinner in need of a Savior, and that Jesus died and rose for me.

Admitting—I couldn't work my way into heaven even as a "good" person. Without a Savior, I was headed for hell.

Believing—that Jesus Christ was the final atoning sacrifice for my past, present and future sins, that He would forgive me no matter what I had ever done, that He would love me no matter what.

Repenting—of my sins, asking for forgiveness. "Repenting" isn't a word we use a lot these days, but it just means we're sick of those sins and want to turn away from them. Another way of looking at it is saying, "Enough is enough!"

Asking—Jesus into my heart, so He could wash me clean from my sins. "Asking Jesus into my heart" is just another way of saying we dedicate our life to Him, promise to follow Him. It's almost like a wedding ceremony, where we say "I do." Only difference: God doesn't do divorce. It's us and Him, forever!

Receiving—eternal salvation. Through Jesus, I was washed clean so I could gain access to a Holy God, the Creator of the universe. I'm headed for heaven and an eternity with Christ.

That's exactly what happened when I was saved. And by the way, If God is speaking to you right now and you would also like to ask Him into your heart, ask Him right now! You can also read through the additional resources at the end of this book and pray to receive Him right where you are. He will listen, guaranteed.

CHAPTER 13

BY GRACE ALONE

For it is by grace you have been saved, through faith—and this not from yourselves, it is the gift of God— not by works, so that no one can boast. For we are God's workmanship, created in Christ Jesus to do good works, which God prepared in advance for us to do.
(Ephesians 2:8-10)

I had to admit that I felt a little strange, standing there in the baptismal pool at Central Community Christian Fellowship in Riverside, in front of all those people. Here I was thirty-nine years old and about to get baptized again, a year after making my decision to follow Christ.

I had already been baptized as a baby in Cuba. It was what everyone did back then. This time, though, it was not because of traditions, but because I myself wanted to celebrate my newfound faith in Jesus. Not because I had to, but because God had simply been too good to me and I wanted to share His goodness with others.

Even so, I could have been shaking a little—and not because the water was cold.

"...And have you trusted the Lord Jesus, given Him your entire life?"

Had I? I faced this question in a more formal way as Pastor Eric Denton rested a hand on my shoulder. He would ask the same questions of everyone who wanted to be baptized.

Yes! There was no doubt. God gave me a deep-down assurance of my new status as His child. The doubt had dissolved, and I knew I would now spend eternity with Him. So that's what they meant in that old hymn, *Blessed Assurance* (Fanny Crosby, 1873). And it didn't stop there.

Since coming to this fellowship, God had showered me with the kind of peace I'd never known before. I had learned more and more about my Lord Jesus under the teaching of Pastor Eric, and I had begun to grow spiritually.

Would I follow Him the rest of my life, and claim Him as Lord? *Yes.* Of course yes!

"On your confession of faith, then, I baptize you in the name of the Father, the Son, and the Holy Spirit."

So I was dunked, and I have to say that water had never felt so good. I was washed clean, a new man. And I knew how blessed I really was as I stepped out of the pool, dripping with water and smiling.

Of course, it didn't end there. Because now I had even more questions to answer—big ones. Even as the waters of baptism dried from my head I was starting to see how I needed a greater purpose for the second (and best) part of my life. I was looking for more than a business, I was looking for *significance.*

But what did that mean, exactly? It meant I wanted to make a difference in the lives of my family, my friends, employees, customers, suppliers... even strangers. I wanted something *great* to do, something I could look back at someday, and know that God was pleased.

It would take a while to figure out, though, even though my perspective had begun to shift from the inside-out—from a self-centered life to a God-centered life. It had changed radically. And for the first time ever, career wasn't ruling my life anymore. Instead, God came first, followed by my family... and *then* work.

But at first I thought everyone who had money and who truly decided to follow Jesus had to donate everything they owned and move to someplace like Ethiopia to do missions work. Well, I honestly did want to follow God wherever He took me. But Ethiopia? And in poverty? I wasn't so sure, and neither was Peggy.

On the other hand, I thought, maybe the Lord wanted me to be a pastor, or a missionary. Wasn't that the ideal way to serve? I wasn't sure, but still I tried to be open to what God had in mind. As I sincerely prayed about this every day, I asked Him, "How can I serve you?"

And pretty soon He gave me his answer, though it wasn't quite what I'd expected.

See, everyone knew how much I enjoyed creating and innovating. I loved building companies, taking something from good to great. I knew how to do that. And I wondered if maybe God would give me another opportunity to work in business. . . Only this time he would get the credit and glory, instead of me. I kept praying for direction.

And as I prayed, it was amazing how God gave me a new heart for people who had never heard the good news of Jesus. People who didn't know what would happen to them if they were to die that day. After all, I knew from firsthand experience what it was like to live life lost. And I think because no one had ever shared the gospel with me for the first thirty-eight years of my life, I sensed more and more the urgency of telling people what God had done for me. Now I knew what I'd never understood before: Making a choice for Jesus was a matter of life or death. A personal emergency. I had to share the secret that God had revealed to me: Jesus!

But. . . how? I still wasn't sure when it would all come together, but now I had a pretty good idea what I wanted to see happen. Among other things...

I wanted people to have the assurance of their salvation. That through faith in Jesus, we are given mercy and grace no matter what sins we've committed in the past or present.

I wanted people to know the up-close and personal God, not a distant and judgmental God I thought used to exist.

I also wanted people to experience a better, fuller life—here and now. Who wouldn't want that?

I wanted people to be set free. And of course there was only One who could buy us out of slavery, who could break our connection to sin and all the junk of this world.

I wanted to share with people the solution to their problems and give them an everlasting hope and option: eternal life.

I wanted people to experience the freedom I had received from Christ, the daily grace. No more guilt, no more worry, no more fear of God. Just the sweet taste of his incredible mercy, grace and love (Three things we don't deserve!).

I wanted others to know the same hope and promise of the future that I had received. Something great to look forward to.

I wanted as many as possible to receive salvation, just like I had. No matter what else happened, that was the bottom line.

I hoped that wasn't too much to ask. But still I prayed. And one day while filling my tank at a local gas station, I looked around at the other people around me and saw a car full of teenagers. I'd been there, too, twenty years before, and I knew who they were just by how they acted. Chances were good that many of them did not know the Lord. And if they didn't, they were on their way to hell. Period.

All of this hit me as I stood there, frozen, wondering. My heart went out to them, and the gas pump started beeping to tell me my tank was full. But still I wondered: Who was going to tell these needy people about the Lord Jesus?

How about me? As soon as I answered that question the pieces of my puzzle started to snap together. By that time I'd been praying for about a year, asking God how I should best serve Him. And as I drove away from that gas station I understood that maybe I didn't have to travel halfway around the world to share the good news.

Not long after that incident one of my best friends from high school, John Gonzalez, called me on the phone to tell me of his brother's sudden death. John broke down, and we both sobbed in grief. But John needed to know the hope I had. What could I say to him?

The answer came the next week while John was at our home, even though I panicked at first when John asked me, "How does a person get saved, Aurelio?"

I could feel the fear and doubt run through me. Could I actually lead another person to Christ? Didn't I first need have to be a trained pastor or something like that? What if he asked me something I did not know?

John stared at me, waiting for answers. Waiting for me to lead him to Christ. I did the only thing I could think of—I ran to the phone and called Randy Thompson, who of course had first introduced me to Jesus.

Randy graciously calmed me down and gave me some quick

coaching on what to ask and what to say. I hung up the phone, still shaking a bit. But by God's grace, that day my best friend John surrendered his life to Jesus. And that experience marked my beginning of leading people to Christ.

Wow! I could share the gospel, and right where God had placed me. I knew that people were dying without any hope or promise, right in my own backyard, right now. But now I understood that God had given me a gift—a burden for those people in the next lane. And by the way, isn't it strange how some Christians can feel led to travel to distant faraway lands to do missions work (which is great!)… but how easy it is to forget that people in our hometowns are dying and will go to hell, as well?

Still I faced another unsolved part of the puzzle. For a long time I anguished whether I should best serve God in a full-time Christian ministry, or in a more secular line of work. I prayed a long time over this, but the doors to ministry never seemed to open.

Yet during this long period of praying and waiting on the Lord for what to do next, God was giving me example after example of how the mystery of God is Jesus Christ, and how people in general had no clue why Jesus came to earth. Jesus didn't come to condemn the world, as people might think, but to *save* the world—and that's the mystery. I needed to let the world know about the saving grace of Jesus.

So on I prayed: How do you want to use me, God? Certainly not in business, right? As a new Christian I worried that no one could fully serve God in a secular operation, in the corporate world I'd come out of. I was afraid that dealing with money matters was somehow not spiritual enough. A cut below.

Good thing God was patient with me. It took a while, but eventually I realized money is not negative in itself—and neither is a call to serve God in a business setting. The real problem was a *love of money*. As the Bible puts it, *"For the love of money is a root of all kinds of evil. Some people, eager for money, have wandered from the faith and pierced themselves with many griefs."* (I Timothy 6:10)

I didn't want to go down that path again. God had set me on a new one, after all. Yet I still arm-wrestled with a crazy kind of guilt, feeling bad for wanting to serve God through business.

I admit it: I yearned to have another business, to know that I had a place in His work and His economy, using the gifts and talents He gave me. I even toyed with the idea of developing another consumer product, and after working on it for a year, I knew it could have been another home run.

Another business? Everyone knew where that had once taken me. But I could do it right this time, putting God first and following a Biblical management style. Or so I thought.

Thinking about the opportunity made me nervous, though. I prayed that I wouldn't slip into reverse, back into the haze of what I'd been and how poorly I'd acted at Dogloo. I knew I had tried to bargain with God during those Dogloo years, looking for money and success from Him. If I performed, if I was disciplined, if I was smart… would He bless me with riches? No! More than anything, I never wanted to focus on what this world had to offer. Not anymore!

So there I was, stuck between two extremes: Certain that God had great plans for the future, but still a little afraid of stepping into a place where the past could repeat itself. All I could think to do was to keep praying, begging for God to have His way in my life. Above all, I didn't want to backpedal toward that time when human tradition, basic principles of this world, and sin wrote my life's focus and headlines.

Actually I did continue to wrestle with the sin issue, since it had left me with a lot of baggage from my old way of life. As a new Christian I had even stumbled through periods of doubt about my salvation. How could I be saved, I wondered, and yet continue to sin against God? How could I mess up and claim to be a believer? Why did I still have problems to deal with? I often felt like the biggest sinner of all. I needed to lean on the truth of Scripture, like in this verse: *"Here is a trustworthy saying that deserves full acceptance: Christ Jesus came into the world to save sinners—of whom I am the worst."* (1 Timothy 1:15)

I wasn't the first one to wonder about sin and doubt—but that didn't make it any less gut wrenching. As I started to soak up God's Word, I heard the call to live by His standards. At the same time I was even more aware of how far I fell short. Talk about guilt.

Like a self-appointed judge and jury I kept convicting myself for every little thing that was wrong with me. I believe Satan did his best to remind and accuse me of every sin, as well, since he's the father of lies and the great deceiver.

Before long my sins started to choke my growth as a Christian, and when I kept tripping over them I wasn't getting much done for the Lord. The shame of my sins kept me from doing any good for anyone. Instead of accepting that I was forgiven, deep down inside I decided I was not worthy of God's grace. And by entertaining that mindset, I gave it that much more credibility. My doubts kept me from growing closer to God, while it kept Satan happy. I couldn't keep this up.

Finally one Sunday afternoon a good friend and fellow Christian, Alvin Davis, noticed my long face while we were at a beach party. When he asked how things were going, I couldn't hide it any longer. I told him how bummed, how burdened I was about my many shortcomings.

"Brother," he told me, looking me straight in the eye, "you have to let that go, now. There's no condemnation in Christ Jesus."

He was referring to Romans chapter 8, where the first verse tells us: *"Therefore, there is now no condemnation for those who are in Christ Jesus, because through Christ Jesus the law of the Spirit of life set me free from the law of sin and death."* (Romans 8:1-2)

But I needed a little more prodding, a little more encouragement.

"Do you understand this, Aurelio?" asked Alvin. "Do you believe this?"

I wanted to. But I kept thinking back to what it was like when I was growing up, when guilt was my friend. Back to the days when I could always spend time in the guilt universe of my mind. As a perfectionist, the guilt I grew up with would haunt me for years, even after becoming a believer. Years before I had even once heard a group of Cubans say, "We are just like the Jews—to feel guilty is a good thing."

And I had so much to feel guilty about. I had entertained my guilty thoughts about doing drugs. I'd held on to my guilt about lust, guilt about selfishness, guilt about my pride and greed. I had even found a way to feel guilt about my guilt. And naturally my guilt always condemned me, keeping me away from a loving God.

As we talked there on the beach, I found what Alvin understood. More importantly, Jesus understood. And that day was the beginning for me of truly accepting God's grace, knowing I didn't have to (and could not) earn any of it. I finally began to understand that His grace brought me the kind of peace I was looking for. That grace wasn't just given at conversion, but was now available for everyday life, for imperfect people like me. And I would find another verse in the book of Ephesians that helped me put the sin issue into focus:

"For he chose us in him before the creation of the world to be holy and blameless in his sight. In love he predestined us to be adopted as his sons through Jesus Christ, in accordance with his pleasure and will—to the praise of his glorious grace, which he has freely given us in the One he loves. In him we have redemption through his blood, the forgiveness of sins, in accordance with the riches of God's grace that he lavished on us with all wisdom and understanding." (Ephesians 1:4-8)

There it was, so simple. Grace. It's all about grace. My eyes were spiritually opened when I finally understood these truths. I realized how God saw me, a sinner, as holy and blameless only because of my faith in Jesus.

As the waves crashed nearby, I came to understand more fully from God's Word how His grace had swept away the shame of Satan's constant accusations—what had led me to so much condemnation. That truth would change how I understood my sin struggle. And I realized at the beach that day how I could never follow Jesus in my own strength. Imagine that! I had always thought I needed to be at a church service, sitting in a pew, to learn from God's words.

Of course, even after that seaside revelation I still experienced what it was like to fall on my face. I knew I could still stumble. As the apostle Paul put it, *"So I find this law at work: When I want to do good, evil is right there with me. For in my inner being I delight in God's law; but I see another law at work in the members of my body, waging war against the law of my mind and making me a prisoner of the law of sin at work within my members. What a wretched man I am! Who will rescue me from this body of death? Thanks be to God—through Jesus Christ our Lord!"* (Romans 7:21-25)

The difference was, now I didn't have to crash and burn all the time, carrying the burden of guilt that disables so many of us. I realized on a daily basis that imperfect people just like me, people who believe in Jesus, are covered by His grace. And grace is receiving what we do not deserve. I learned that God's power and grace could overcome my weakness to sin... if I just let Him.

As a reminder I turned to Romans 8 again and again. There I read how, through Christ Jesus, the law of the Spirit of life really had set me free from the law of sin and death.

I compared that truth to the Old Testament experience, before the time of Jesus. We read Old Testament stories of how people lived and died by how well they could stick to the law. Back then, everyone who broke the law had to sacrifice their way back into fellowship with God. So it was one sacrifice after another, and they were going through the motions.

I could certainly understand that kind of situation. Because after a few years of walking with Christ, after several years of stumbling over and over again, I realized I was just like the people in the Bible. For them, routine sacrifices eventually became rituals, and rituals came to have little or no meaning. Looking back at when I had tried to do more good than bad, I remembered the temporary feeling of "I'm okay... for now."

But God wasn't very impressed with people who just went through the motions, and He hadn't been impressed with me, either. From the outside, you might have compared such people to polished caskets, shiny and spotless on the outside. But on the inside? Just dead man's bones.

That's why I was so grateful for the beach party reminder that I could never earn my position with God. The more I had tried to please God, the clearer my failures had become. And the dead-end that had kept me away from Him ended right there by the sea.

So if the Old Testament was about how people fell short of keeping God's standards, the good news in the New Testament turned out to be how Jesus fulfilled the law for us by His death and resurrection. If God had not given Jesus as the one and only sacrifice for mankind's sins, we would have had no hope. But the sacrificial death of Jesus untied us from the law, so we could be freed by grace, not bound by law. Today, now that Jesus has come, the law is good for exposing sin and leading us to the cross. That's what I learned— God's solution to man's sin tendency.

Now my motive would be to please Him as a friend, not as a reluctant slave who has no choice but to follow the rules. I felt a new power, like a strong wind, clearing the air. I thought, *I'm free now!* Forget the tyranny of sin and death.

Grace alone. I sure didn't deserve this. Who did? Yet as believers, we become part of His family, so we have His grace-filled attention when we come to Him every day.

From then on, I began to sense more and more how things worked with God. I had to leave my past mistakes to Him, let go of my current mistakes, and allow His power to bring me His peace.

The choice was clear. Going forward, I was either going to depend on my power or His power.

Yet at one point I still remember wondering, *If we're always saved, do believers have any right to sin? Even a little?* The apostle Paul asked, *"What shall we say, then? Shall we go on sinning so that grace may increase?"* (Romans 6:1) To answer that question, God led me to the book of Ephesians. That's where Paul talked about grieving the Holy Spirit who brought us to Jesus and sealed our souls. *"And do not grieve the Holy Spirit of God,"* he wrote, *"with whom you were sealed for the day of redemption."* (Ephesians 4:30)

Clearly the Holy Spirit of God grieves. I was reminded of that fact during a great sermon I heard some time later at my weekly Bible study (Bible Study Fellowship International). God actually grieves. Isn't that a compassionate, awesome God? Yes, but I also found that our God would much rather know us and spend time with us—not cry for us.

So once again I wondered… knowing I was totally forgiven of my past, present and future sins, could I just keep sinning? No way! God had been too good to me. Knowing that He sacrificed His Son for my sins made me not want to sin. And I did not want to continue offending my family and friends with my past mistakes, so how could I now offend God with a careless lifestyle?

I concluded that sin doesn't fit into the equation. Not even a little. I think that answers the question. It all came back to the cross. This new life was now possible because of Jesus and His work on the cross. And the new freedom I discovered on the beach had nothing to do with anything I had done—or would ever be able to do. But speaking of what I would do, I still had a question to answer: Ministry, or business?

Or both?

CHAPTER 14

BY FAITH, NOT SIGHT

*By faith Abraham, when called to go to a place he would later receive
as his inheritance, obeyed and went, even though
he did not know where he was going.*
(Hebrews 11:8)

For years I had ridden dirt bikes in the high desert near Victorville, California, and I'd never once stopped for anything other than to get gas or to eat. This December evening in 1999 was different. After a day of riding, my son JR was nearly driving me crazy wanting to visit a skate shop. So, I agreed to go. While driving home through Victorville, we stopped. The skate shop happened to be right next door to a tiny little store called Christian Head Shop.

Excuse me? I thought head shops were places where people bought drug paraphernalia. So I was pretty confused about the "Christian" part until I poked my head inside to check it out.

Oh! This was a Christian-run shop that sold cool T-shirts and other witnessing tools, with bass driven Christian music booming through the sound system. They were definitely spreading the Gospel through their merchandise, but in a very cool way. I'd never seen anything quite like it. A woman named Kelly greeted me.

And right away my mind started racing; my business instincts began to kick in. I started asking Kelly (who turned out to be the owner) all kinds of questions, like…

Who are your customers?
How long has the store been open?
Where do your suppliers come from?
Do you make a profit?

Maybe I was jumping into this interview a little too quickly. I could tell Kelly didn't have a clue why I was so curious. She couldn't tell I'd already envisioned a nationwide chain of stores just like the Christian Head Shop.

"So you like the idea?" she asked me. And I guess the question caught me off guard. Sure I did, but what did she mean? Well, I didn't know what else to ask her, anyway, so after telling her I liked the store I introduced myself, shook her hand, and headed out for the door. Interview over.

"Aurelio?" she asked, and I had to stop. With a name like mine, I was used to that question.

"Right." I spelled it out for her. A-u-r-e…

"No, Aurelio." She didn't want me to spell it, after all. "We used to get high together on the railroad tracks, remember? What, about twenty… twenty-two years ago?"

I stopped and looked at her again, trying to remember. By this time she obviously recognized me.

"Remember?" She asked again. "It's Kelly!"

Oh, wow. I was blown away by what she—and God—were telling me. A face from the past, another story of being redeemed, this unique little shop… this was too much. I found out that she and her friend owned and operated the little store as a ministry, a way of reaching out to the unsaved in their community. And after talking with Kelly a little more I had to jump into my truck with JR and head for home. I couldn't wait to tell Peggy, so I got on my cell phone and told her everything that had just happened.

Were all these things just coincidence, or was God finally answering my prayer? I wasn't sure at first. But Peggy knew the answer just like that, right away.

"Of course it's from the Lord," she told me, without hesitating and without a shred of doubt in her voice. "What do you want, Aurelio, a billboard sign from the Lord, right there on the freeway? Maybe with your name on it, telling you exactly what to do next?"

Well, that would have been nice. But really, I knew Peggy was right. And deep down I also knew God seemed to be opening an incredible new door for me here. This was how I would be sharing His life changing good news—the grace, truth and love of Jesus. And I couldn't get this idea off my mind.

I would wake up every day, wondering if this was really what God wanted from me. I would fall asleep praying about the same thing. I started to work up a business plan to open a chain of relevant Christian apparel stores—not just to sell clothes, but to spread the gospel. And eventually I felt His approval, His hand on me as we worked up this plan to open Christian stores for young people all over the U.S.

God was in this.

Again it reminded me of Thomas and his weak faith. I'm like him a lot more times than I want to admit.

Now, Thomas was a personal disciple of Jesus and witnessed boatloads of miracles. Even so, he always asked for more and more evidence. After Jesus died and rose on the third day, even after Jesus appeared to other disciples, Thomas still wouldn't believe it. Remember his line? *"Unless I see the nail marks in his hands and put my finger where the nails were, and put my hand into his side, I will not believe it."* (John 20: 25)

So a week later the disciples (including Thomas) were together in the upper room they had rented for the last supper. And even though the doors were locked, all of a sudden Jesus was right there with them, making himself at home. He knew how Thomas was having a tough time with the whole resurrection thing. So He told Thomas to go ahead and poke away, prove it for himself.

"...Stop doubting and believe," Jesus told him. Thomas, as you can guess, was impressed.

"My Lord and my God!" He said, and we can still hear the "Wow!" in his voice, even from this distance of years. But of course that wasn't the end of the lesson. Jesus assures Thomas that *"...blessed are those who have not seen and yet have believed."* (John 20: 24-29)

Even though Jesus was talking to Thomas, when I read this part of the Bible story it sure feels as if He was talking straight to me. So the point here is that we're not alone in our disbelief. Unfortunately, it runs deep in our nature. I can tell you that from personal experience.

But look at the apostle Peter, one of the Lord's right hand men. After the crucifixion he ran away from the cross, back to his nine-to-five job on the fishing boat. Jesus had to go looking for him all over again.

Same with us: We pray, and we receive. *And we still question the Lord.*

Even so, I still entertained those nagging little doubts, Thomas-style. After all, the idea didn't make much business sense, at least not on the surface. Starting a store from scratch was a very iffy proposition—especially since this retail concept had never yet been proven. Sure, everyone knew about the thousands of other Christian stores—but none were aimed specifically at youth.

So I prayed for months; I wanted to be obedient to God's leading. I really did. And the more I prayed the more I understood that even through all the uncertainties, I could not run away from this thing. God seemed to be bringing it to my attention every day. One very large practical question remained, though: Who would supply all the Christian youth products we would sell? And how could we open a Christian retail store for youth with virtually no suppliers? As far as I could tell, these kinds of suppliers just didn't exist—yet.

Once we accepted that the suppliers were limited, that pretty much left us with one option: We would have to make our own products. This understanding eventually led us to create our own clothing and accessories brand which was totally uncharted territory for us.

So the deeper we researched, the more questions we uncovered. Like, how big of a market would there be for Christian clothing, and for youth? We had no idea. If people bought their first "Christian" shirt, would they ever come back? Good question. And what exactly made this Christian clothing, well, *Christian?*

Whew. Although I could see the pieces coming together in a lot of ways, we still faced a lot more challenges than we did open doors. I knew from having been a manufacturer (who sold a ton of Dogloos to retailers, remember) that retailing was a rough road. I'd heard all the horror stories and they kept popping up at all the wrong times fueling discouragement.

And yet I actually started to think that maybe we could be looking at the next generation of Christian stores. Maybe this would be different. Maybe this could work in a way that others hadn't. Of course, if it was ever going to fly, God would have to launch it, not me. I kept praying.

It was at about this point that Satan really began digging in to discourage me. It wasn't hard to tell what was happening. Even some of my closest Christian friends thought I had gone off the deep end.

"Christian stores for youth?" They would ask me. "Are you out of your mind?"

Well, maybe I was. Another friend in particular asked me how much cash I was going to put into this project, as if to find out where my limit was going to be before I would wise up and get into something else, something more serious.

That kind of reaction got me down, but God protected me from their good intentions. I knew they cared about me, and I also knew they had not received the same calling. But not everyone was down on the idea.

My sister Sonia encouraged me to go ahead—but carefully. I trusted her advice, as she had played a huge role in our success at Dogloo. So the two of us ventured ahead, slowly and cautiously, even though at first we actually thought we were developing something more like a Christian skate park. She and I drove all over Los Angeles for months, interviewing other related Christian businesses. Anything was possible at this point.

But I wanted to be sure, and so we researched Christian stores, and we researched skate parks that were the rage at the time. We attended Christian music festivals, and spent a lot of time attending youth outreach events. This was a tiring process, but it had to be done. I needed to do my due diligence.

This is when I began to realize that everything in my life

was coming together, like the Bible says, *"for such a time as this."* (Esther 4:14) Everything I had ever done—all my challenges and struggles in life—led me to this point. I could understand the pain and heartaches of being young, and the totally lost feeling that came with not having a godly compass. I figured my first hand experience of being a lost youth myself would help us deal with non-Christian customers, and understand where they were coming from.

I also knew what it was like to chase (and catch) the things this world offered and I knew the allure of money that really couldn't buy me happiness or peace.

Most of all, eventually I knew the Lord Himself led me to this idea of a Christian store for youth. He'd taken away the dead emptiness and instead given me a drive to share the answers and the hope that had taken me thirty-eight years to find. Now all I wanted was to pass along this mystery of God and introduce this Jesus who loved me and had given all for me.

We had to find a good name to describe what this journey of faith was all about, though. Something catchy but also something that boiled everything down to a word or two. So one day I was working on my computer, puzzling over the concept. A techie friend of mine, Alfonso Chavez, asked, "How about you abbreviate the Colossians 2:8 scripture into C28?"

When I heard that, I knew it was clever and simple. Perfect! And after much prayer we settled on Alfonso's suggestion of C28 ("C-two-eight"), short for Colossians 2:8, where the apostle Paul warns his friends: *"See to it that no one takes you captive through hollow and deceptive philosophy, which depends on human tradition and the basic principles of this world rather than on Christ."* (Colossians 2:8)

Still, I was not done with the names. I actually had to choose two names—one for the stores, and another for the clothing line we would introduce. I stayed awake many nights praying and asking God for help.

"What do you really want to call this thing, Lord?"

The C28 scripture tie-in really spoke to me, since I'd once been swept away in the world's spiritual tsunami. I had been a slave to human traditions and the things of this world in my past life and in my past career, and it had left me empty and broken. But now the clothing line… I was stuck.

While driving down the 91 freeway, I asked Peggy for her ideas. It didn't take long. She answered me with a big smile.

"Not of This World," she said. "Are we not?"

I thought, *yes, yes, yes! Perfect! We are not of this world. I get it!*

The most incredible thing about these two independent phrases ("C28" and "Not of This World") is that when you paraphrase the entire Colossians 2:8 scripture, you really get the idea that we are "not of this world," and it's "all about Jesus." So everything flowed together, even though each idea came independently, through two different people. With much prayer, everything flowed together.

Talk about answering prayers.

So C28/*Not of This World* fit exactly what we wanted to say, and it matched what we were all about. And at this point I knew God was definitely leading. After about a year of research and prayer we decided to move ahead with the mall concept. We figured if C28 was going to be effective in reaching the lost, it was going to be in malls, where secular people could actually make a decision for Christ any day of the week.

The mall? I knew all about the financial risks of locating in a mall. For one thing, the sky-high cost of rent could eat us alive. But God would have to deal with the money issues. I just wanted to give people a choice, a taste of something totally different from the mainstream stores. Besides, in many cities, the mall is still the center of youth culture and the heart of the community. We figured that opening clean and positive C28 stores in malls could put us in front of fourteen to sixteen million visitors each year.

Millions of visitors! I couldn't think of a better opportunity. With C28 I imagined reaching thousands upon thousands of unbelievers with the good news of Jesus, all in a non-threatening and relevant way. These would be people who never imagined stepping near a church. People living empty and hopeless lives, just like I had been doing for so long. People who were headed to hell without Christ, and did not know it.

With C28 we were going to meet them like Jesus did, right in the public square, right where they lived their everyday lives. Because although Christians are warned to not to be *of* this world (plugged into it for our strength and motivation) in the same Scripture we're also called to be *in* the world. That means we can't hide and we can't shrink away from the opportunities God gives us to share our hope. So there's a crucial difference between *in* and *of*, and C28 is all about living that difference.

Well that's great, but this story had just begun. The next obstacle: How to actually set up stores in malls. We found it's actually harder than one might think, in part because most mall management companies don't exactly want Christian stores occupying space in their properties. Too controversial for them, they said. Too risky. Sorry. It actually got to a point where the malls wanted nothing to do with us—as if negotiating with a Christian store might be against the law.

I'm a little ashamed to admit how relieved I was at having this door slammed in my face, at first. In fact, I was somewhat relieved at the thought that I might actually be off the hook with God. I told Him, "You know what's happening here, Lord. If you want me to go ahead and make this happen, then you're going to have to clear the way. You know I've done all I could."

I had done everything I knew how to do. And now I could only inch ahead in prayer and in my trembling faith. Because one thing I understood, even back then: God knows how much we can take before He rescues us.

CHAPTER 15

THE WALLS CAME TUMBLING DOWN

*The seventh time around, when the priests sounded the trumpet
blast, Joshua commanded the people, "Shout!
For the LORD has given you the city!"*
(Joshua 6:16)

Eventually it didn't matter much what kind of roadblocks the malls put up, or what reservations they might have had about renting space to a bold Christian store. The Lord opened our first door in 2001 at the Tyler Mall in Riverside, California. That first C28 opened only after I, my sister Sonia, and friends Andrea Law and Roger Thompson fasted and prayed for 40 days. That's no typo. These dear people seriously sought God with me.

Week after week, we fasted for seven-day periods each. We believed in what God had called us to do, so we fasted to get closer to God and to hear from Him. We desperately needed His answers. Even so, at one point I considered trying to get off the hook.

Okay Lord, I thought, *I tried. And it looks like the doors are closed.*

But on the morning of the day 40, the phone rang.

"Mr. Barreto," I heard a voice tell me, "we have no idea how this happened, but there appears to be a spot available for lease."

Well, I had an idea how it happened. I knew then it was all about praying, waiting and trusting in the Lord's sovereignty. When God began opening doors, they swung wide open. And as we tripped through them, I was constantly reminded of God's faithfulness, His strength, and His direction. Over and over I repeated a verse I'd memorized, probably because it seemed like a perfect theme song every step of the way: *"What, then, shall we say in response to this?"* Romans 8:31 reminded me. *"If God is for us, who can be against us?"*

On the surface, it seemed like just about everyone was against us. As we made plans to open our second store in Orange County, California, a large real-estate group approached us with an offer. Good news? Maybe not. Once the mall owners found out that C28 was a Christian store, they refused our application to enter The Mission Viejo Mall.

Later, also in Orange County, South Coast Plaza told us that C28 didn't fit their marketing mix or marketing plans. Once again we'd been denied. As a Cuban-born immigrant I had never experienced discrimination of any kind in my life until I began doing God's work as a Christian. At that point, I knew I had a legal right to contest their decision based on discrimination laws. But we did not challenge either management group, instead giving the decision up to God and wading into yet another 40-day prayer session. By this time our designer Abe Hernandez and District Manager Sarah Buffington were on board, so as a C28 team we asked God for His solution, not our own. At the end of this second session of prayer, God immediately answered by instead opening doors at The Promenade Mall in Temecula.

Once again, we experienced God in a much more powerful and intimate way by giving Him the room He needed to do even bigger things than we could have imagined. In the process, I learned another lesson about trusting God. Because I stepped out in faith and straight into God's gracious arms when I personally guaranteed a 10-year, $1 million dollar lease at the Promenade Mall, even though I was trembling at the time.

We hadn't turned a profit at our Tyler Mall store, where the surrounding population (over a million) was more than double that of Temecula's. On paper this might not have looked good. But I held on to Jesus, and I often asked God to protect me from my own mind—and Satan's doubts.

So what happened? When we opened in Temecula, sales zoomed over the top. In fact, they doubled what we projected, and all praise goes to God.

But God didn't leave it there, because not long after that He opened the door for us to sponsor our first Christian concert… right there in the mall. We could hardly believe it when, in the rain, over 5,000 people came—and many received Christ as their Savior. Since then we've sponsored concert after concert at the Promenade Mall, with up to 10,000 people attending.

What are the chances? Jesus said, *"With man this is impossible, but with God all things are possible."* (Matthew 19:26) I hung on to this promise.

The key here is understanding that only God can deliver these kinds of results. But first we have to believe. That's probably the hardest thing to do as humans. Believe like a child would believe? Not easy. Trust that God has your best in mind? Well…

We thought of that when we started lining up our third store, this time at the Main Place Mall in Santa Ana. Three days before opening the store, one of our main Christian suppliers announced they would no longer sell us their brand, period. What? This supplier told us that doing business with C28 stores in Orange County would label them as a Christian company, and they wanted to avoid that.

Obviously I was shocked. Jolted. Floored. C28 stores had promoted this Christian brand for months, and now…. Well, legally, we felt they had no right to stop selling to us. I even considered court action to force them to come through with the products we needed, but again turned it over to the Lord after praying and talking with my pastor, Milton Vincent. We agreed that Christians should not sue each other, as Paul advises in 1 Corinthians 6. So I placed this whole mess in the Lord's hands, wondering what would happen.

Initially we lost a lot of money when they stopped our supply of merchandise. This was no surprise there. But what happened next was amazing. Numerous complaints about this clothing company and their advertisements suddenly began to roll in. After much discernment, we thought the complaints were valid. But here's the thing: through God's hand, we were delivered from being associated with this supplier. In other words, God was looking out for us. And the lesson here? Trust God's plan, not the plans of other people, not our own plans, not the ways of this world. *"Trust in the Lord with all your heart and lean not on your own understanding; in all your ways submit to him, and he will make your paths straight."* *(Proverbs 3:5-6)*

The fourth and fifth stores, located in Escondido and El Cajon, were a gamble, so to speak, by the world's standards. At one point our Escondido store was losing $5,000 month and we were almost ready to close it down. Who wants to lose that much money when you can donate that to another ministry? In spite of the financial hardships at C28 Escondido, by faith we marched on into San Diego County to open our El Cajon store. And wouldn't you know it, El Cajon did wonderfully, way above our expectations.

I have learned through experience that the more room I give God, the more I see God's work—and it is much better than mine. That's because our God is always gracious and faithful. I'm reminded of that fact every day as many people come to C28 stores to pray, and I hear back from them. In fact, we could probably fill this book with just the stories of customers and others whose lives were touched by God in a C28 store.

One of the earliest redemption stories came from the Escondido store, the day after it opened. That's when a rough-looking young man walked into the store with a "666" tattoo on his hand, which was intimidating. So he asked Tim, our store manager, what C28 was all about and where the ideas came from.

Of course that was the right question, as Tim began sharing the life-changing gospel message of the grace, truth and love of Jesus with this visitor. And an hour later the young man broke down sobbing as he realized he was not living for anything that would last. Tim asked him if he was ready to repent of his past sins and place his trust in Jesus Christ as Lord and Savior. The young man looked at Tim with a longing in his eyes.

"Yes."

Yes! The Bible says that angels rejoice when sinners are saved. Well, there must have been a party in Heaven that day, but that was just the start. Later on, the young man's older brother came into the store, wearing the same from-the-pit-of-hell "666" tattoo. Tim almost panicked as the man walked right up to him and looked him straight in the eyes.

"What have you told my brother?" the man demanded.

Oh no, thought Tim, *I'm a dead man.*

But he wasn't, at least not yet. What seemed to be the problem?

"I've never seen him happier," the man told Tim.

When Tim was finally able to breathe once more, he spent the next few minutes sharing the gospel with this man, too. And finally the tough guy wanted to know something:

"Can I have this, too? What my brother has?"

*As a matter of fact...*Tim must have smiled at the question as he introduced this seeker to the Lord, just as he had with the guy's brother.

What an incredible day—and it didn't stop there. Because here's the most amazing thing of all: thousands of people have since placed their faith in Jesus Christ at that Escondido store alone, and that has been worth all the financial struggles we have endured.

I would estimate that nearly a third of C28 customers are alternative customers, like the brothers with the tattoos. They're secular people, tired of mainstream brands, and they're looking for something different. Most haven't heard of the real Jesus, don't know what He stands for, and don't yet believe in His redeeming grace.

So we're here to make introductions, and then step back to let the Spirit of God do His work. We're here to share the life-changing gospel message of grace, truth and love found in Jesus Christ. That message is truly not about this world, but all about the Lord we serve. And our people will tell the story any way we can—through what we sell, or what we can say.

In fact, the majority of our products in C28 stores points consumers to the truth of the Bible, whether it's alternative Christian clothing ("witness wear"), music or accessories...

That's great, but C28 stores are different not just because of what's on the shelves. They're different because our priority is sharing the gospel. Anyone who works for us knows that talking to others about the Lord is a major part of the job. They need to be comfortable explaining Bible verses on shirts and connect it to the design.

Being comfortable with praying aloud for people is also expected of our store employees. Some customers come into our stores just for prayer. And many of those customers tell us how refreshing it is, how different to be approached by people who really care and who will pray for them.

Of course, sometimes we have to challenge our staff to excel in the name of Jesus, but that's part of the ministry, as well: to teach them an honest day's work, working as unto the Lord. Remember what Paul told the believers in Colossae? *"Whatever you do, work at it with all your heart, as working for the Lord, not for men..."* (Colossians 3:23)

In the process, we obviously have to keep an eye on our bottom line or everything will come to a grinding stop. Our stores have to make a profit to stay in business and push us toward a much greater goal: saving souls.

But wait a minute: Isn't this a ministry? It actually took me a while to feel right about requiring that we make a profit. But I know profits are a good thing, because they help us grow the outreach. Without sales we cannot survive as a business that also ministers to people.

Little do people know that an ordinary day of shopping could bring the best transaction of all, salvation through Jesus Christ. One hundred percent of the credit and praise goes to our mighty God.

By God's grace, I keep everything in perspective. I am a Christian businessman with a calling to have both a for-profit business and a ministry. I have to balance paying all of our bills all the while maintaining focus on the mission of sharing the gospel through apparel and evangelism.

So… ten years after the first C28 store opened, we're still in malls sharing the gospel. By His grace and provision, over 16,000 people made a decision for Christ through our stores, our outreach concerts, speaking engagements and even through C28.com and our clothing brands *(Not of This World, Truth Soul Armor and Canvas)*. What a mighty and gracious God we have. It goes to show you that with faith and obedience God can move mountains.

Good thing, too. Because I was just about to face one of my biggest mountains, ever.

CHAPTER 16

IN SPITE OF
CIRCUMSTANCES

Trust in the Lord with all your heart and lean not on your own
understanding; in all your ways acknowledge him, and
he will make your paths straight.
(Proverbs 3:5-6)

Not long after I had decided to serve the Lord through C28, I found myself on my knees by the side of my bed, sweating, praying, and pleading with God in fear.

"Why now?" I asked Him. "What have I done wrong? Aren't you pleased with me?"

God didn't answer right away; He just let me sweat as my nest egg drained away, minute by minute.

No, I wasn't the only one losing money in 2000 and 2001, when the stock market took a terrible nosedive. But we had most of our assets invested in the market. Satan knew where to attack. I remember all too well the feeling of panic, shock, and helplessness as I lost 40 percent of my net worth in a matter of days.

Just like that.

The thing I had worked for my entire life—my earthly security— was evaporating and there was absolutely nothing I could do about it.

It still saddens me to realize how often and how much I have depended on this world for comfort and security. I know this is my greatest of many "thorns." The apostle Paul had them, too. *"To keep me from becoming conceited because of these surpassingly great revelations,"* he wrote, *"there was given me a thorn in my flesh, a messenger of Satan, to torment me. Three times I pleaded with the Lord to take it away from me. But he said to me, 'My grace is sufficient for you, for my power is made perfect in weakness.' Therefore I will boast all the more gladly about my weaknesses, so that Christ's power may rest on me."* (2 Corinthians 12:7-9)

This is what my sin nature does: It's like I know what is right and I know what is wrong, but I do what is wrong. I worry and fear when I know better, almost as if to say, "Sure, Lord, I know you're in charge. But this is a really big problem. I don't think you can help me out of *this* mess."

After all, those days of the dot-com bust were horrible. I had trusted my resources over to a Harvard MBA money manager who, even with all his wisdom, could not predict the future or control the present. I had placed my faith and trust in the stock market instead of placing my money safely away, and I had bet on the stock market with 60 percent of my assets in high risk companies.

How could I make so many mistakes? I wondered.

Never mind that history would repeat itself in years to come. God's wisdom in Proverbs 3:5-6 *("Trust in the Lord with all your heart…")* began to take hold in my life. That's because even though I had often tried to engineer my own success—before and after we started C28—I discovered just how many times my best plans didn't turn out to be very good ones at all.

In other words, what I thought really ought to happen, or what I thought would happen…often did not. And that's still true today. As each year passes I see more examples of how this works, and I see more and more evidence that everything I thought I knew… doesn't really amount to much.

I imagine a lot of Christians can identify with this kind of thinking, even if they're not running a business. How often do we think the circumstances are awful? And how often does God have to show us that He's in charge, not us? At the same time, how often does He have to prove that He's for us, and that He's taking care of us 100 percent?

Unfortunately for me, it was always easy to lose sight of His blessings when I forgot to believe in His promises and instead inadvertently chose to listen to the enemy's lies and doubts. Too often I forgot to praise God for His blessings and instead just dwelt on how things *didn't* turn out my way. After all, it's an old habit of mine and tough to break.

On the other hand, the sooner I leaned on Him and trusted Him completely, the more peace He gave me in return. I found it was a great trade. Even in the face of uncertainty, confusion or trials, I found this is when my witness is the strongest. This is when God sharpens my testimony for Him. This is when my faith grows the most.

So now when the business seems ready to drown me or when the future looks overwhelming, I no longer waste time fussing. Because it never fails: The sooner I let go, the sooner I see His hand sweep through each circumstance. The sooner I surrender to His will, the sooner His peace sweeps over me. The sooner I turn my worries and concerns over to the Lord, the sooner He shows me that He has already thought of everything.

This is where Proverbs 3 comes into play, when the path I've charted for my family, for myself or for the company seems totally straight and headed in the right direction. Sometimes my plans turn out to be totally crooked. But what does the Bible say? "... *and he will make your paths straight.*"

However, there's a condition here, and that's the first part of the verse about trusting in the Lord with all your heart. Did I trust the things of this world, or did I trust Him? I constantly have to remind myself that when things do not go according to my plans, God is right there, ready to straighten them out for me, through trials.

But I still need to surrender my problems and plans to God, allowing Him room and time to step in. That's the key. That's when He actually makes the much-needed changes.

So out of that stock market mess I learned one more time to cling to the finished work of Jesus. There was no other way to escape the snare—He had to die for us. And He was the only one who could snatch me away from my sin and my sin nature.

I praise God for Jesus and I praise God for choosing me out of the rubble. Especially the rubble of the stock market crash. Because I know, beyond a shadow of a doubt, that I couldn't have survived that event without Jesus.

Before Christ? I would have literally melted down, since the security that money represented to me was all I really valued. I'd worked myself into a frenzy trying to grab it all and then to hold on to it. It's sort of like the sad old Gollum creature in the *Lord of the Rings* story, who wanted the powerful ring more than anything else in the world. If "Precious" (the ring) was taken away then Gollum would have nothing left to live for.

I was just like Gollum, only my "ring" was money. So today I'm thankful for what happened, if you can believe that.

Honestly, the crash was the beginning of understanding firsthand that the things of this world could never give me the real protection and security I needed. In a way that I'd never expected, the crash moved me closer than ever to Jesus, to love Him and trust Him even more. When the world's old security blanket was stripped away, He was there like no one else could be. And now He is still there, as I know He will always be.

It is said that God's power resides at the foot of the cross. Now I know how true that is. The foot of the cross is where we meet Jesus, where we get to know the power of the gospel to totally transform our lives. Not just save us, but to transform us.

But I really didn't begin to understand that deeper truth until my pastor, Milton Vincent, shared it with me over lunch one day. When you place your trust in the things of this world, he told me, the things that you have will eventually (and inevitably) let you down. Everything changes in life, he said, but God never changes. Systems will let you down, people will let you down, but God will never let you down.

"Begin trusting God 100 percent," he told me as we ate. "Not trusting in what you have."

How I needed to hear this. Had I followed his wise advice earlier, perhaps I could have avoided a lot of pain. As it was, losing millions of dollars had brought far too much grief to me and to those around me. My poor Peggy.

Even then, I held on to fear. Fear of what the stock market crash could do to me. Fear of investing in a new concept like C28 and *Not of This World.* Fear would not leave me completely for some time. More on that later.

For now, though, Pastor Vincent patiently showed me how God could transform the way I did business, from sales and marketing to operations and customer service. Milton showed me how the gospel was available for everyday living. And I did want to learn. Because even in loss, I would find that God pours out mercy through the grace we find in Jesus. In other words, the same power that wiped away my sin and saved me for eternity in heaven—that same power would totally refurbish my life—if only I would let Him.

It all breaks loose at the foot of the cross. It breaks loose right through the pages of the Old Testament, because everything in that part of the Bible leads up to Jesus, just like all of the New Testament is about Him.

The sad part is, too many people think the cross is just their ticket to heaven, period, end of story. That it all stops there. I knew very well that too many people pray the prayer, believe they're saved, and then just go on with their lives the way they'd been living before. I could tell you all about that.

But I had been so wrong. Because even though salvation was my starting point, I would learn that there's so much more. After all, the gospel is designed to turn our lives upside-down. And so the ongoing power of the gospel is available to those who seek Jesus, who surrender their everyday circumstances to Jesus, by the hour and by the minute.

I would find that God's power for totally transforming lives and for everyday life is ready for release when we seek Him and His grace through daily prayer. God wants us to experience the gospel benefits everyday. And once more, it all flows from the foot of the cross.

The cross and the Bible also remind us where we came from, how we're sinners and deserve hell as our penalty. But through Jesus we get forgiveness instead. How fair is that? Let's keep things in perspective. We're obviously not perfect, all-knowing, or sinless. So we can forget about whining and complaining, and we can be thankful for the things we do have. It's only from a place of humility that we can rejoice and praise our loving and merciful God, the way they do in heaven all the time.

For me, it was so comforting to understand and to begin to know in my heart that I bring nothing to the party, except my faith in Jesus. Yes, the little faith I have in Jesus, in God the Father, is enough to save and to keep a wretch like me in His grace. Praise the Lord!

Here on earth we get to praise Him ahead of time, even before heaven. We get to thank Him ahead of time. And He wants us to fully experience Him in our everyday lives, in our everyday business. When the stock market crashes and housing market collapses, or when things seem to be going great…it doesn't matter.

In fact, we can actually find complete fullness in Him while we experience life's circumstances and challenges under His sovereign Lordship. We can find our lives at its fullest when we're at our lowest point only if we submit to Jesus. I wish I would have learned that sooner. The apostle Paul says it much better than I ever could, and every word applies to the person who would succeed at life, or in business: *"…and to know this love that surpasses knowledge—that you may be filled to the measure of all the fullness of God. Now to him who is able to do immeasurably more than all we ask or imagine, according to his power that is at work within us, to him be glory in the church and in Christ Jesus throughout all generations, for ever and ever! Amen."* (Ephesians 3:19-21)

So here's the treasure: All we have to do is remember what it was like back when our lives dead ended in sin. We deserved hell, but instead we got amnesty from God, His forgiveness, and His undeserved favor. It hit me when I was celebrating my eighth year after my salvation: *This could have easily have been my eighth year in hell had I not given my life to Jesus.*

The hand of Jesus pulled me out of the gutter and cleaned me up, but not to just go back to how I once was. Never! He has great plans to use me for His glory. To live life fully, no less. And no matter how rough the road seems, I know and take comfort in the fact that He's in control.

Born again, saved, believer, converted, come to faith, faithful... however you want to describe it, we've inherited His blessings when we accept Jesus Christ as Lord and Savior of our lives. We inherit His kingdom through our faith in Him, and He is pleasured by this. We didn't earn God's mercy and we sure didn't deserve the grace of Jesus, but nonetheless, we have it. He showered His grace and favor on us, and we may never fully know the why or the how.

When we think on all that, we can't help but to move ahead— from complaining about life's bumps and life's losses (even stock market crashes) to appreciating His grace, His favor. Sure, we're aware of life's troubles. We can see as well as anybody when business is down, when our kids are in trouble, when our health declines, or when our marriages need help. But now we can surrender all that to Jesus every day, every hour, every minute. He promises to bear our load, and He does when we truly surrender it over to Him.

These were the kinds of things I began to see when Pastor Vincent set me straight over lunch. I didn't learn them all right away, but I began to see a new business plan and a new blueprint for real success. I started to see then that the next time I faced business losses, or the sales projections didn't work the way I planned, I just had to remember for a moment where I'd be if I got what I really deserved.

I still need to remember the transaction Jesus made when He died and rose again, and what that means for my life and work today. I need to remember on Whose coattails I'm riding, and how small my troubles really are in the grand scheme of it all. Financial difficulties? It's all how you look at it. And then I just need to recognize where my real hope comes from, in life and business.

From the foot of the cross.

Aurelio at the family ranch
house in Cuba 1962.

Boys never grow up.

Peggy teaches Aurelio how to drive his first ride, a stick shift!

Peggy and Aurelio get married in 1980 at age 21.

Aurelio and Peggy buy their first home in Inglewood California
at age 21.

Peggy, Baby and Story inside the first of many doghouses Aurelio
builds before inventing Dogloo.

The Barreto family at home in the early 90's (L-R): JR, Peggy,
Hilary, Aurelio and CoLene.

Achieving the American Dream. Aurelio sits on top of the world at
Dogloo. 600 employees, $62M sales -$8M in earnings.

Aurelio and Peggy at a fundraiser after the sale of Dogloo.

C28 Stores' first outreach concert in 2001. Five thousand people attended and several gave their lives to Jesus Christ that night.

CHAPTER 17

TRIALS OF GRACE

No temptation has seized you except what is common to man.
And God is faithful; he will not let you be tempted beyond what
you can bear. But when you are tempted, he will also provide a
way out so that you can stand up under it.
(1 Corinthians 10:13)

Imagine me sitting in front of my computer late one night, struggling to write my first letter to all those faithful C28 supporters. These were people who had recognized the vision, who had believed God, and who had faithfully stood behind us in this work of faith.

Faith—I felt I had so little of that. And now God was asking me to communicate with thousands of these wonderful people. Yet my fingers hesitated over the keyboard, as once again the doubts swept over me. I thought about what I was doing, and about what I needed to say.

But how could I? I had never been to seminary; I wasn't very well schooled. How could God use a person like me? How could a sinner like me have the nerve to lead this evangelistic movement? What did I know?

Not much. I figured there had to be plenty of other people better trained and more qualified. For sure just as many more who loved the Lord better than I did, people who had a much better track record with Christ. Did God have the right man for the job, here? I felt like Moses when he had asked God, "Why choose me?" Something just didn't add up.

But it did, in God's economy. As I struggled with that letter I remember dropping to my knees, feeling overwhelmed as I realized how patient and gracious God was being with me through this whole process. As the tears fell and as I wept in humility over God's choice to use a sinner like me. I prayed in repentance over my failures, as the man of faith I thought "I should have been by now."

And then I recognized that God had a habit of using the lowly for His purposes. I was lowly, no doubt. So it hit me just how compassionate God truly is, and how He could use anyone—no matter how low—for His good plans. Even people like me who had lost millions of dollars that could have been used in the ministry instead.

You see, about the same time I was losing millions in the stock market crash of 2000, I also found myself pouring millions into C28. I know that sounds odd. But if it were not for God's leading, His promises, and His grace, I certainly would have stopped building C28 at that point.

I didn't fully understand what was going on, though. It's not hard to do the math: Part of the money I lost in the market crash was the very same money I had already set aside for starting C28.

"What's going on here, God?" I had asked.

I thought it was a good question. At the time, I have to admit I was pretty confused, and I had very few answers. All I could lean on was the fact that God was (and is) sovereign. He gives and takes away as He chooses, in all areas of our lives, and for our own good. Remember King Solomon's words? *"When times are good, be happy; but when times are bad, consider: God has made the one as well as the other. Therefore, a man cannot discover anything about his future."* (Ecclesiastes 7:14)

Looking back, I can see how God was teaching me the truth of this verse, even as He taught me not to depend on my bank account. But that's much easier to say now than it was then. Back then the prayer and support from wiser Christian friends kept me from pulling the plug on the ministry.

My wife Peggy of course always kept me in prayer. I can't adequately express how much that has meant to me. And although they were younger at the time, my kids CoLene, JR, and Hilary also prayed faithfully for me. What a blessing! I believe God listened to their prayers for strength. I could actually feel it.

So never mind all those financial speed bumps we hit during the early years at C28, and never mind all my doubts and feelings of inferiority. God gave me a special gift at the time—the courage to be faithful and persevere. This too was His grace. There's no other explanation.

I credit Him with an enormous amount of grace and patience and me with none. Because at first I didn't own the faith I would need to continue pouring time, talents and treasures into the ministry. That kind of faith was a clear gift from God's hand—God's gift of grace through trials.

Look at what happened through all the trials in our business situation, beginning with the loss of much of the funding meant for investment and start-up. But never mind. God seemed to ignore what we thought were huge hurdles, and the results have been so far beyond impossible, a work of God. Because He kept us on His life-support, tens of thousands of lives have been changed for all time. And I know there's more to come.

Sometimes even now, though, it's hard to follow what God is doing, and how, or especially why. But one thing I do know: Somehow, and for some reason, God has given me great favor. There's no other explanation for the flood of grace He continues to let loose on me, each day. He lets me experience all the good things I don't deserve.

Today we're a long way from that first uncertain letter, and we communicate with over 200,000 people through our C28 email lists, and over 150,000 people on Facebook. How about that for a loving God? He could pull this off, no matter how weak we are or how broken our lives. And I'm not just talking about C28.

We've also been praying about my anxieties and depression, which I've been battling my entire life. I remember being only five or six years old and feeling depressed, like a dark cloud was hanging over my life and I couldn't break free. I felt depressed sometimes in high school, and even entertained thoughts of suicide. And I've battled anxieties as an adult.

But after years of praying, reading and working on my anxieties and depression, things started to change. In fact, after coming to Christ my anxiety and depression were literally cut in half. This was a huge bonus for me and my family at first, though my anxieties didn't totally disappear.

Sure, I'd always been pretty good at hiding my fears in public. But Peggy could see right through me, like no one else. She knew exactly what was happening. For years she wanted me to seek medical treatment for my mood swings. As an adult, I found they were better than before. But still they persisted.

I resisted Peggy's pleas for me to get help because I was too stubborn and prideful. I felt that I would be less of a Christian if I went for *that* kind of help. If only I would pray more often, I thought, things would get better.

But Peggy would not give up, and she finally helped me see how my depression wasn't just a personal thing, anymore. It was a physical condition that affected her and the kids, too. So, I relented and went to see a doctor.

Even then I prayed a lot and searched for the best advice about what to do. And after trying a few different medications, my mood swings started to lessen. At age forty-five, I was freed from a lifelong bondage of anxieties and depression. They haven't disappeared completely, but I'd say an 80 percent improvement is quite a blessing.

I actually had no idea how much support I would receive from my other brothers and sisters in Christ when I simply told them I was on medication. God was gracious, as always—and so were other Christians. I quickly came to realize that my medications for depression and anxiety were really no different from the cholesterol medicine I took for my heart, or ibuprofen for headaches.

My only regret was that it took me so long to seek treatment. It's amazing how much time I lost by putting off getting medical help because I wrongly thought it wasn't the Christian way. Somehow it wasn't spiritual to seek help, I thought. All that wasted time just gave Satan opportunities to attack me through my depression.

So for anyone who has battled depression or anxiety—anyone who has already tried prayer, counseling and exercise—I strongly recommend getting medical help, as well. If not for yourself, then for your family. Because I know from personal experience how God can use doctors.

There were many doctors and many trials with different medications. It was a good friend that finally got me the right medications for my anxieties and depression, by recommending I see a psychiatrist who was better able to diagnose and prescribe the right medications for me.

In fact, I felt God's hand and His grace during the entire treatment process. God is good, even when everything looks hopeless. He is good in the middle of the worst business crisis or family trial. He is good in the deepest pits of despair or depression. And He is good no matter how intense the trial.

God is good, period.

CHAPTER 18

THE LORD IS NEAR

*Consider it pure joy, my brothers, whenever you face trials of many
kinds, because you know that the testing of your faith develops
perseverance. Perseverance must finish its work so that you
may be mature and complete, not lacking anything.*
(James 1:2-4)

Do trials fit into the normal Christian life? I once thought that trials would disappear when I accepted Christ. But in fact, after coming to Christ and accepting the job of starting C28... my trials intensified.

I would need a calculator to count how often C28 has been accused of being worse than thieves for retailing Christian products, or slandered for simply being a Christian retailer. The most hurtful attacks came from the Christian community itself, with comments falsely accusing us of everything from "fleecing the flock" to "taking advantage of God."

People questioned why we are in malls, or accused us of not looking like a Christian company. They didn't understand our deepest desire to reach the lost for Jesus, and how lost people happen to frequent malls.

The criticism raises questions, though. As Christians, what are we supposed to look like? Are we to disassociate ourselves completely from the world? Not at all. Jesus was clear about being in this world, but not being part of this world. He said, *"My prayer is not that you take them out of the world but that you protect them from the evil one. They are not of the world, even as I am not of it."* (John 17:15-16)

Jesus spoke with and hung around with the lowly, with the disenfranchised. Jesus had a heart for the lost and He knew that to reach the lost, He had to go to where they were at. I believe He would have gone to the mall. He is our role model.

Jesus called us to be that bright city on a hill, to be the light for all men to see. *"You are the light of the world,"* he said. *"A city on a hill cannot be hidden. Neither do people light a lamp and put it under a bowl. Instead they put it on its stand, and it gives light to everyone in the house."* (Matthew 5:14-15*)*

So we are not of this world, because Jesus is our world. He is our light and we must share Jesus everywhere we go, and in all that we do.

Yes, those critical comments were hurtful. And the first to throw stones was often the the legalistic, Old Testament type of Christians that have little understanding of grace. They spend far more time looking for what they perceive to be sin in others rather than doing what God tells us to do first: *"How can you say to your brother, 'Brother, let me take the speck out of your eye,' when you yourself fail to see the plank in your own eye? You hypocrite, first take the plank out of your eye, and then you will see clearly to remove the speck from your brother's eye."* (Luke 6:42).

Despite the stone throwing, though, with God's help we have stayed the course. By God's grace we have witnessed many changed lives. Kids and adults who were once suicidal or about to give up all hope, have now instead given their lives over to Christ. Now they're not just alive, but on fire for the Lord Jesus. Many new believers are now actually leading others to Christ themselves.

In fact, through God's wonderful grace and His Holy Spirit's power over 16,000 people have prayed to receive Jesus Christ as their Lord and Savior in the past ten years through the ministry of C28 and *Not Of This World.* And we praise the Lord almighty. This is amazing grace, despite the attacks and the trials.

The Bible actually has many examples of how God uses trials and difficulties to build a person's character and to bring them closer to Him. That's a good thing. I'm living proof.

But… is it disappointing to hear that we should expect tests, trials and challenges? That may not be the rosy message of some modern TV preachers, but it is the message of the cross, it's found in the Scriptures, and it was preached by our Lord Jesus. Look at what He went through.

Who invented the human goal of not having any trials, of skating through life with as few scratches as possible, whatever the cost? That's not a Biblical approach. Still it's interesting how we always ask each other "How was your day?" or "How did it go?"

And then the other person explains all the circumstances, as a sort of rating system.

Yes, it's good to show that we care about another person, but I'm afraid those questions only reinforce the idea that our joy should depend solely on what happens to us from minute to minute.

See, if we focus only on our circumstances, we live and die by our circumstances. Circumstances are always temporary, anyway. It's a life in the flesh instead of a life in the Spirit. On the other hand, if we focus on the Spirit, we live in the Spirit. So the Bible shows us a better way: to be Spirit-driven and faith driven, not circumstance-driven.

What if we ask instead "How was your day with the Lord?" That would bring us to a more significant level in a hurry. That would steer us away from focusing on circumstances. We can see that while life may be a series of trials, it's the way we deal with trials that determines our joy and peace.

I know from experience what it is to go through trials with God and without God. How about if we take a look at both options, just to compare…

Option A: Without Jesus I was totally alone to face life's challenges.

How good is that? Option B: Today I know I'm never alone. I've found I can do all things through Him who strengthens me.

So this is your multiple choice quiz. Which option sounds like a better life deal?

I know many times I have been on my knees pleading with God to rescue me from situations that may have seemed hopeless, situations where the business had no visible solutions. I've also seen that God never gives us more than we can handle. This truth always applies to every decision-making dilemma, business or personal.

Sometimes the process hurts, though. I had to plow through a whole lot of pain before I fully surrendered to His will and received His comfort. But even surrendering to God's will still hasn't kept my sinful nature from wanting to rear its ugly head. All I can say is that we are all surely a work in progress.

At times I cried out, "God, is this the way you want me to feel?" And quickly my anxieties faded away. Even so, I realized how stubborn and prideful I can be. I absorb way more pain before I get back on track with Him. Even though I know better, I still keep trying to do things on my own (in my flesh, in my power) and not using God's resources (in the Spirit, in His power). This is my sinful nature—the one that only leads me into trouble.

That's the downside. The upside is that in the first ten years of my journey as a Christian, I grew more in my inner being than in my first thirty-eight years of life. And this growth has always been paved with trials. Now I see trials are a normal part of life, and many times God engineers trials to get my attention or bring me closer to Him.

From previous chapters you already know that I lost my

country as a child and grew up poor. I've battled depression my entire life. I lost my business after building it for ten years, then lost millions in the stock market crashes. The first five years at C28 were a financial disaster, and some months we lost $50,000. My wife and I have had rough times in our marriage. The list goes on…

But today I see those trials in a completely different light. Although I would never have believed it before, I know now that one by one, they have actually brought me to completely depend on my Lord and Savior Jesus Christ. And for that, I am totally grateful.

Oh, I still struggle with sin, just like any other Christian. I know what is right, but I do what is wrong. I often do what comes natural in the flesh rather than in the Spirit. The fact is, all of us have done things we know we shouldn't have done, and we regret it. But thankfully, God is still full of mercy.

One of my favorite character studies from the Bible is King David. He is very easy to relate to, since he committed just about every sin in the book—and there were times when his problems just about consumed him. But in times of need David always turned to God for help. He had a repenting heart. And the Bible says that God loved him!

No one is immune. We can all find ourselves in that same grip of hardship. What did David do? When he was overwhelmed, he cried out to God for help, over and over again. In writing, even, as Psalm 13 says: *"How long must I wrestle with my thoughts and every day have sorrow in my heart? How long will my enemy triumph over me?"* (Psalm 13:2)

Sound familiar? Good thing the king didn't end it there. Because here are the final lines of this praise song: *"But I trust in your unfailing love; my heart rejoices in your salvation. I will sing to the LORD, for he has been good to me."* (Psalm 13:5-6)

Did you notice how David rejoices in his salvation in the above verse? Remember who is our salvation? Jesus is our Salvation, our Savior. When we focus on Jesus, I mean really focus and meditate on Jesus, instead of our circumstances, the sheer power in his name JESUS releases the supernatural power of the Holy Spirit to bring phenomenal peace and joy. Try meditating on Jesus over and over again, and wait on the Lord for change.

When we are face to face with heavy burdens, God is always there for us—whether we decide to believe this fact or not. So we can choose God's way... or we can put Him off. The truth is that God is the only One who can answer prayers. And it is through answered prayers that we know He is there.

I learned my lessons the hard way, during the toughest years of the business. David learned his lesson the hard way, too, and he learned that consequences follow sin like a shadow. But ultimately God always forgave David, because David learned how to repent, how to turn away from his mistakes. In fact, he agonized over his sin as he asked God to forgive him.

"I will exalt you, O LORD, for you lifted me out of the depths and did not let my enemies gloat over me. O LORD my God, I called to you for help and you healed me. O LORD, you brought me up from the grave; you spared me from going down into the pit. Sing to the LORD, you saints of his; praise his holy name. For his anger lasts only a moment, but his favor lasts a lifetime; weeping may remain for a night, but rejoicing comes in the morning." (Psalm 30:1-5)

David knew those nights of crying his eyes out. So have I. But the amazing thing is that we can know the same God that David cried out to. Is this the God that you know? Get to know Him. Reading and thinking on Psalm 30 is a great place to start.

Even before David composed Psalm 30, he had already seen a full dose of God's power. Everybody knows the story of how God gave David the strength to kill Goliath with a single rock. He was just a kid at the time.

We have to remember that David didn't manage that feat on his own, though. He knew where the strength, the aim, and the results all came from. David knew God's power just like he also knew God's favor was clearly upon him.

And yet, here's the frustrating part: David spent the next several years running away from King Saul, who wanted David dead for making him look bad. You can read all about it starting in 1 Samuel, chapter 19. So here's David, running and hiding in the desert, afraid the king is going to find and kill him. Remember, this is David, the same guy who had already known God's clear favor. Even so, God had to take David through a desert of despair before making him king in Saul's place. Can you identify at all with what David went through? I sure can.

In fact, three of David's psalms have been huge encouragements for me: Psalm 142, 143, and 144. The words have blessed millions of other people, too. It's easy to empathize with how David is feeling in this Psalm: *"I cry aloud to the LORD; I lift up my voice to the LORD for mercy. I pour out my complaint before him; before him I tell my trouble. When my spirit grows faint within me, it is you who know my way. In the path where I walk men have hidden a snare for me. Look to my right and see; no one is concerned for me. I have no refuge; no one cares for my life. I cry to you, O LORD; I say, "You are my refuge, my portion in the land of the living."* Listen to my cry, for I *am in desperate need; rescue me from those who pursue me, for they are too strong for me."* (Psalm 142:1-6)

David wrote those words when he was hiding in a cave, afraid for his life. And again it's a good thing they don't end there: *"Set me free from my prison, that I may praise your name. Then the righteous will gather about me because of your goodness to me."* (Psalm 142:7)

We may not understand at the time. But if God brings us through trials, He does it for a good reason. Sometimes I see this in hindsight. But the more I experience Him and His ways, the more I see how good they are while I'm in the midst of one.

It helps, though, to bring our problems to God immediately, without wasting any time. That way we sidestep the kind of pain we don't need to bring on ourselves. God wants us to operate this way, too, coming to Him, depending on Him. It doesn't matter how often we've blown it, or how deep our mistakes are. Our all-powerful God can handle it. And it doesn't depend on how "good" we've been. God's mercy and grace are not tied to our deeds.

The fact is, God promises to never leave us. He wants us to come to Him with our fears and our failures, dropping the load at His feet. Oh, and to leave the load right there. That's the way Jesus told people to pray: *"Ask and it will be given to you; seek and you will find; knock and the door will be opened to you. For everyone who asks receives; he who seeks finds; and to him who knocks, the door will be opened. Which of you, if his son asks for bread, will give him a stone? Or if he asks for a fish, will give him a snake? If you, then, though you are evil, know how to give good gifts to your children, how much more will your Father in heaven give good gifts to those who ask him!"* (Matthew 7:7-11)

We can believe that God is going to hear our prayers. When

in doubt or when the bottom falls out, we pray. Even if we look in the mirror and don't like what we see, it's time to pray. Even on the worst of days when everything seems to go wrong and we can't take it anymore, we can pray. Because if we seek God with everything in us, He will show Himself. Here again, this is how we can know He is there and He is God—through answered prayer. He promises to take our burdens from us and give us His peace.

Speaking of burdens, though, don't we tend to forget our blessings a lot more than we remember the trials? We naturally focus on the bumps in the road, forgetting all the smooth sailing. And as soon as we're out from under a nasty mess, it's easy to just look for the next crisis.

King Solomon records a pretty graphic explanation of this flaw in our human nature: *"As a dog returns to its vomit, so a fool repeats his folly."* (Proverbs 26:11)

What a disturbing visual. It's almost as if sorrow and pain become our best buddies sometimes, and we dip down into the pit of hell for a fill-up. Instead we should reach up to God for true joy—the genuine article.

The apostle Paul had a better idea: *"Rejoice in the Lord always. I will say it again: Rejoice! Let your gentleness be evident to all. The Lord is near. Do not be anxious about anything, but in everything, by prayer and petition, with thanksgiving, present your requests to God. And the peace of God, which transcends all understanding, will guard your hearts and your minds in Christ Jesus."* (Philippians 4:4-7)

Worth noting from this passage is that the Lord is near! We cannot rejoice in the Lord if we fail to realize and remember that the Lord is near. And when we finally understand just how near He really is, Scripture starts to come alive. And when it does, the only thing I can think of doing is to thank God.

So relish the trials in life, no matter how painful they appear at the time. Look at them as stepping stones to knowing our mighty God a little better. Now is a great time to thank God for stooping down and working in our lives.

I thought I had already endured the toughest trials, but God was only using those trials to prepare me for more life lessons. I would really have to learn to believe that the Lord was truly near and that I could fully trust Him and find joy in Him *alone*.

CHAPTER 19

JESUS, MY HOPE

He will sit as a refiner and purifier of silver; he will purify the Levites and refine them like gold and silver.
(Malachi 3:3a)

I remember weeping in fear and disbelief as I drove home one night, the disappointing numbers still echoing in my head. How had it gone so wrong?

The last time we'd heard good news had been months ago, back in August 2008. We had celebrated a great C28 "Back to School" selling season and we were praising God. And normally, good "Back To School" numbers point to a good Christmas selling season, as well.

But not this time. The very next month, the great housing bubble burst and the stock market began its meltdown. Now, the encouragement we'd felt back then was a hazy memory, as sales tumbled month after month...

Little did I know that it would continue its downward spiral... *for 17 consecutive months! What is going on?* I asked God. *How can this be?*

We'd had no contingencies against a stock market collapse, or a housing meltdown. This was way over our heads. So we simply did what we knew best: We prayed for God's help, and for His wisdom to help us make the tough decisions and for Him to provide for our needs.

Of course, this was Southern California, and for years California had been going the wrong way. We all knew it. California had clearly become the greatest of entitlement states, and this national downturn had broken the proverbial camel's back. It did not take a rocket scientist to realize California's leadership had taken us the wrong way for years, for decades.

Yet I had lived here nearly my entire life and had never seen real estate prices collapse so quickly—fifty to sixty percent—in such a short time. On a personal level I truly felt like the most naïve of people, losing again what God had given me. I felt ashamed before the Lord. He had entrusted me with great assets and I had inadvertently squandered them.

But God was beginning another chapter, so what else could we do? We simply had to let go and allow God to take care of us.

Don't get me wrong, though. We didn't just sit around "letting the grass grow under our feet," as my sister Sonia had often warned me against doing. We worked hard "as unto the Lord" and did the best we could with what we had control over, and we trusted in God in those areas we had no control over. Do you know what I mean?

Still, I had no answers as I watched most of the assets the Lord had given me ten years before begin to slip away. It was surreal. And I often wondered...

How can I be so stupid and allow this to happen—one more time?

After all, this had already happened to me seven years before, in 2001. And honestly, I never thought it would happen again. But this was just the beginning; what followed was even worse. Like precious silver, God was refining me further.

For me it was a month after the market crash, on a Saturday morning in November. My wife Peggy and I got into a huge argument about my jealousies during a dinner party the night before. Looking back, I can't believe how self-absorbed I acted during this most difficult of times.

But the argument escalated into a perfect storm, and a week

later I was experiencing Thanksgiving in my large house... all alone. Peggy had left.

I could not stop worrying and I could not even eat. (Some people eat when they are stressed; I lose my appetite.) I had never even cooked a meal for myself.

"Why, God?" My question echoed in the big, empty house. "What have I done? I'm so sorry, my dear God."

I prayed for hours alone in my living room, pleading for God to reveal Himself, to speak to me, and to help me. And then around 10 o'clock that night, the phone rang.

It was my pastor, Milton Vincent, calling to check on me. Clearly, the Lord was answering my prayers. And that night I began to learn a huge lesson: God was more than enough for me. I began to realize that if God chose to take away everything dear to me, but I still had *Him,* I would still have it all.

Like Job, I was learning that God was more than enough for me, that God was all that I needed. God would restore my life, marriage, and business whenever He felt it appropriate. And the amazing part? *I was okay with that.* A huge peace began to come to me. My family had been severely attacked by the enemy; my business and my assets were nearly gone. But that night I actually slept easy knowing that God was with me, and with Peggy, in spite of the horrible turbulence of bad news all around us.

But what next? A good friend recommended I get counseling, and quickly. By God's grace I was able to see Dr. Bob Hughes, and incredibly gifted Christian psychologist in Orange County, the next week.

In the very first meeting, though, I could hardly stop sobbing. When I finally did, it was like the Lord began filling me with the Holy Spirit's power. Dr. Hughes kept pointing me to Jesus, and the more I looked to Jesus, the more the pain would go away. It was a very real washing of sins, and I could tell the Lord's grace was upon me. I think I got six hours of counseling that first week.

As it turned out, Dr. Hughes had written a wonderful book called *Love Focused: Living Life to the Fullest*, which I immediately began to read. And as I continued meeting with Dr. Hughes, he started helping me get my priorities straight again. Jesus first—not family, friends or business.

By my second week of counseling, my life goal became clear: to love God above all else and then to love others. I learned I could tangibly love God by showing love to other people. The more I thought about others, the less I thought about myself and the more joy I received.

The nugget of wisdom I cherish most from that book is that if God didn't restore my marriage and took all my assets away, and I only had Him, I had *more* than enough. It was God's approval and assurance (not man's) that made me feel complete. And He *is* more than able and more than enough. God is my source of joy. So once I was able to receive the fullness of God by focusing on Him alone, then I was able to extend His grace fully to others—especially to Peggy.

Still the solo counseling continued, and weeks passed. I learned so much. But what about my wife Peggy?

Finally, after several very long months, I picked up the phone to speak with Peggy for the first time since the trouble began. What would she say? How would she respond? I needn't have worried. To hear her voice was an amazing gift from God. To hear the friendly acceptance was an incredible blessing. I breathed again, though she couldn't see the smile cross my face. Soon, her friendly emails were like precious water to a thirsty soul.

But things were different this time. While I enjoyed Peggy's new fellowship, I began realizing that she was not my cake, but the icing. What I mean is, in times before, I had looked to Peggy to be my everything, and I realized how that had placed a huge undeserved burden on her. I first needed to feed on God's Word and the fullness of Jesus before I would be able to properly receive Peggy. My cake was Jesus, and as long as I was okay with Jesus, then I would receive the icing.

Eventually Peggy and I began to get counseling together with our pastor, Milton Vincent. It was Milton who brought Peggy and I to repentance before Jesus. Milton knew that if we humbled ourselves before Jesus, God would glorify Himself before us. He sacrificially spent countless hours counseling us, and never gave up on us even when it looked hopeless.

So we prayed for help continually and asked others to pray for our marriage, too. And as we slogged through the issues, we came to know that God genuinely wanted our marriage to make it. God truly listens and answers prayers. I also came to realize how much I'd hurt Peggy over the years with my jealousy and insecurities.

Here's how it happened: Peggy and I obviously grew up in very different families. Different countries, for that matter. As you might remember from earlier chapters, I came from a conservative, well-to-do Cuban family—well-to-do, that is, before we lost everything and had to flee and start over in the States. You've already read that story. Peggy, on the other hand, was from a working class family from California. We married at the tender age of twenty-one with no pre-marital counseling and even less Christian guidance.

So our marriage had drifted up, down and sideways over the years, but we'd stayed together by God's grace. I always remembered my dad telling me how he had always been faithful to my mom, how he only ever loved one woman in his life. Early on I appreciated those powerful words, and they served me well.

But the minute both Peggy and I came to Christ in 1998, the battles in our marriage seemed to intensify. I don't mean to shrug off responsibility. But I'm sure the evil one didn't appreciate what had happened to us, and I'm sure he was determined to drag our marriage down. After all, Satan knows that if he can break a marriage, he can break a family. And if he can break a family, he can break a ministry, (not to mention a community). No wonder marriage is one of his favorite targets.

Now, as a Latin male, my jealousy had risen to the top as the primary problem in our marriage. Through God's grace, neither of us ever committed physical adultery, although I had to admit my mind had a habit of lustful thoughts all too often. What did Jesus say about this? *"But I tell you that anyone who looks at a woman lustfully has already committed adultery with her in his heart."* (Matthew 5:28)

Through the many trials in our marriage I came to see how much Peggy truly loved me. Obviously neither one of us was perfect, but we started to find a way to completely trust in God's promises. And we started to see how our marriage could change when I humbled myself. I prayerfully dove into a well-loved section of Paul's letter to the Ephesians: *"Husbands, love your wives, just as Christ loved the church and gave himself up for her to make her holy, cleansing her by the washing with water through the word, and to present her to himself as a radiant church, without stain or wrinkle or any other blemish, but holy and blameless. In this same way, husbands ought to love their wives as their own bodies. He who loves his wife loves himself."* (Ephesians 5:25-28)

I had to learn how to obey this passage, how to prayerfully put it into practice in our marriage. And I found out that when a man loves his wife unconditionally, the way Jesus loves the church, great things would begin to happen. The rips and tears I'd caused in our relationship would begin to mend. Remember that it was the church that actually crucified Jesus, and Jesus died for the church. That's the kind of love Peggy and I needed, and only God could grant it to us. We couldn't manufacture it on our own.

Of course it goes both ways, and we also had to look at this equation from the other angle, as well: *"Wives, submit to your husbands as to the Lord. For the husband is the head of the wife as Christ is the head of the church, his body, of which he is the Savior. Now as the church submits to Christ, so also wives should submit to their husbands in everything."* (Ephesians 5:22-24)

We learned that when a wife submits to her husband, she is actually worshiping God. Certainly it's tough for a woman to submit to a weak and sinful man. Peggy and I knew from firsthand experience how hard that would be. But we also knew that when we both decided to submit to the Lord, the relationship would finally grow as God intended. That's when Ephesians 5:21 kicked in, summing everything up: *"Submit to one another out of reverence for Christ."*

So that was our challenge. Meanwhile, Milton took us through a book called *When Sinners Say "I Do." Discovering the Power of the Gospel for Marriage.* It was through studying this book that I recognized *I* was the number one problem in my marriage, and that if I would first focus on my relationship between me and God, God would take care of the rest.

I had to answer several tough questions: Was I trusting God? Was I relying on God? Was God not in control 100 percent? I needed to give all my circumstances over to God 100 percent. Either God was in control, or He was not. And if He was in control, then I need to let go and stop controlling or expecting situations to go my way. This was so freeing.

It was also a blessing to recognize that my problem was not with Peggy. My problem was with God. At this point I was brought to my knees in prayer, asking God to restore my relationship with Him. And sure enough, God began restoring what the locusts ate for thirty years of our marriage. That's when things truly began to change, but not before we went through even more pain.

Not long after we had begun counseling, I was out driving and received a call from Pastor Milton. I almost couldn't believe what he told me—that it could be a few more months before Peggy could get back together.

What? I pulled into an empty parking lot, stopped the car and began to weep and cry out to God. Months? I wasn't sure I would take it. But I did remember Milton's words that while it was okay to be mad at God, I should also tell Him exactly what I was thinking and feeling. So I cried out to God, and He placed this passage of Scripture in my heart:

"Although you have been forsaken and hated, with no one traveling through, I will make you the everlasting pride and the joy of all generations. You will drink the milk of nations and be nursed at

royal breasts. Then you will know that I, the LORD, am your Savior, your Redeemer, the Mighty One of Jacob. Instead of bronze I will bring you gold, and silver in place of iron. Instead of wood I will bring you bronze, and iron in place of stones. I will make peace your governor and righteousness your ruler. No longer will violence be heard in your land, nor ruin or destruction within your borders, but you will call your walls Salvation and your gates Praise. The sun will no more be your light by day, nor will the brightness of the moon shine on you, for the LORD will be your everlasting light, and your God will be your glory. Your sun will never set again, and your moon will wane no more; the LORD will be your everlasting light, and your days of sorrow will end. Then will all your people be righteous and they will possess the land forever. They are the shoot I have planted, the work of my hands, for the display of my splendor. The least of you will become a thousand, the smallest a mighty nation. I am the LORD; in its time I will do this swiftly. The Spirit of the Sovereign LORD is on me, because the LORD has anointed me to preach good news to the poor. He has sent me to bind up the brokenhearted, to proclaim freedom for the captives and release from darkness for the prisoners..." (Isaiah 60:15-61:1)

The Scripture was comforting, of course, but the follow-up news from Milton a few weeks later was only more disturbing. He wanted to prepare me for the reality that Peggy and I still had a lot of work to do, and that we might not be able to get back together for another six months.

That's obviously not what I wanted to hear. From my despair once again I fell to my knees and cried out to God, and again God answered my prayers. I heard from reading His Word that *I did not have to know how, and I did not have to know when, but I knew that God would take care of my burdens.*

From that point, God's wonderful grace and peace began

to flow through me like never before. I came to know that whatever happened, I was okay with God, and whatever He had planned for my life was more than okay for me. I was filled with His incredible peace and joy. It had taken unexpected pain, but I had finally been freed from the torments of my circumstances. At age fifty, I was finally beginning to experience a genuine Christian life; a fullness that came from God *alone* and not from circumstances.

The peace had finally come. But it had taken brokenness before God to bring me to a place of total and complete dependence upon Him. This was the place where I needed to actually exercise my faith, to put my trust into action. In the process, I found three pillars to build upon.

The first was *faith* based on the knowledge of God's Word. The second was *believing* the things I knew to be true. And the third was *trusting* Him by waiting upon Him.

The good news, though, was that after all those struggles and questions, after all the tough lessons, and after months of counseling and hard work, the Lord *did* restore our marriage completely. It's all by His wonderful grace. I tell people today that I actually enjoy being around Peggy, instead of just loving her the sacrificial way that we are taught to love our spouses. She is my girlfriend, and we are rediscovering the fun of being married.

I know that God chose Peggy to be my wife, and we're blessed as a couple by the grace He's draped over each of us. He is the one who repaired and strengthened our relationship, for the better, and for His glory. As we've celebrated our anniversaries, every year we're able to thank God and praise Jesus for His grace. Once more, we don't deserve it, but what a gift. I love Peggy dearly.

Did I say it wasn't easy, though? It took months after coming back to our home and living together for these realities to start becoming real. But I began loving Peggy, not out of duty, but out of desire. How? By finally listening to God and by learning to look at marriage from His perspective. Here's a checklist, some of the most valuable lessons I learned...

It's not about me. To fully experience marriage the way God intended us to, we need to understand that marriage is all about God, developed by God and therefore sacred to God. A thriving marriage is always a great glory to God because it displays a clear and selfless attitude of placing our spouse's needs before our own. It displays Christ's abundant grace, and it reminds us how Christ died a selfless death and paid the price for our mistakes and sins. So when we die to ourselves and our personal desires, placing our spouse's needs before ours, we can truly experience the gospel. And what we truly think about the gospel of Jesus Christ... is what determines the success of our marriage.

If we can humble ourselves and realize that we are actually the number one problem in our marriages (and our spouse isn't), that's when God begins to bless our relationships. That's when our relationship with God blossoms, as well. You see, our biggest problem is not our spouse; our biggest problem is us—and our relationship with God.

So please take an honest look at yourself. If your marriage is broken, first ask God to reveal what is broken in your relationship with Him. Ask God to reveal the sin in your relationship with Him, before pointing fingers at your spouse or anyone else. Do you get this?

Realize that sin is in each one of us and therefore in our marriages. Don't be consumed with our spouse's imperfections; ask God to reveal your sin so you can repent and be the spouse He wants you to be. For years I made my spouse out to be responsible for my sins, foolishly failing to look to the everlasting source of all joy, Jesus.

Marriage means sanctification. Did you know that spouses are strategically chosen by God to reveal the sins and imperfections in our lives? Yes, marriage is one of God's great instruments to bring us closer to Him. Not that we can't be close to God if we're not married. But marriage can be His tool of sanctification. And sanctification is the work and process of the Lord, cleansing us more and more as we become more like Christ. Our spouses can serve as great instruments of sanctification, revealing more of our sins.

So when we finally understand how the greatest problem in our marriage is ourselves, we can then begin to love our spouse without expectations, the same way Jesus loved the church and died for her. And the way we treat our spouse reveals how much we truly love God. I will say this again, in all humility: When we finally recognize ourselves as the greatest problem in our marriage, we can then begin to truly live in grace, and pass that grace along to others. Wow!

In doing so we need to be quick to listen to God, and quick to forgive our spouse. But if our focus is on God first, then we can love our spouse unconditionally because we will be completely full of God's grace and not lacking anything.

One caution. If we have not come to grips with our own sins, we cannot see our need to receive the grace of Jesus daily. And if we do not receive grace, how can we then forgive and offer grace to others? But once we understand our failures before a perfect and holy God, we can begin to grow in grace, and offer grace to others who do not deserve our grace. What is grace? Grace is about giving favor to others who don't deserve it, just like God gives us.

Strands and consequences. Another "relationship" verse Peggy and I both love is from the book of Ecclesiastes in the Old Testament: *"Though one may be overpowered, two can defend themselves. A cord of three strands is not quickly broken."* (Ecclesiastes 4:12)

The best thing about this verse is that our third strand is Jesus. He is our center that holds us together, and we're bound to Him as we are to each other. And one thing is for sure: Without Jesus between us we could not love each other the way we do.

It saddens me to know that for some people it's too late. An ex-spouse may have already remarried and have another family. But remember the truth of God's promises:

"And we know that in all things God works for the good of those who love him, who have been called according to his purpose." (Romans 8:28)

Never forget that God still loves you. Search the Bible for what God is saying to you. Repent of your sins and obey His teachings, and He will bless your future. He promises to do that, no matter what's happened in our lives or our relationships. God always forgives us through Christ.

That's the good news. The not-so-good news is that unfortunately there are always consequences to our actions, and they usually affect others. Broken relationships always leave debris, like rocks on the freeway that bounce up and hit us in the windshield.

That's why it's a good idea for husbands and wives to protect their marriage by praying daily for their marriage. It's naïve to assume everything is okay as we fall asleep at the wheel and allow the enemy to bump us off the road. Fight for your marriages and for your families. Be proactive. In this area we always need to be awake and aware, just as the Scripture tells us: *"Be self-controlled and alert. Your enemy the devil prowls around like a roaring lion looking for someone to devour."* (1 Peter 5:8)

Well, I'm always in prayer that the enemy will stay out of our marriage. I'm determined, because God has blessed us with three great children who deserve a godly home. And I can already see His grace flowing in the lives of CoLene, JR, and Hilary.

Of course, as with anything but especially with kids, mine require much prayer. That's always true, from infants to young adults. Yet it still amazes me that when Peggy and I are proactive in prayer, God does amazing things for us and our children—ahead of time. Is that like a pre-emptive strike? He always listens and helps us. He is faithful. So I've already started praying for my kids' future spouses.

Love and respect. Men want to be respected and women want to be loved. I know that's a generalization. The problem is, men do not deserve to be respected, and women do not truly deserve to be loved. Why the contradiction? Because deep down in our sinful flesh each of us was born with a selfish desire to place ourselves first. And when we place ourselves first even above God, we inadvertently worship ourselves. Can you believe it? We actually prefer to worship ourselves rather than the one who created us in His image. This is that very sin nature that we are born with; even the best of us subconsciously place ourselves not only before others, but before God Himself.

In much the same way, when we lean on our spouses to fill the deepest emptiness in our lives, we inadvertently make them out to be idols. And you know what God thinks about idols. The number one commandment is: *"You shall have no other gods before me."* (Exodus 20:3)

So I should have known better. But for years I had looked to my spouse to replace my emptiness and my shortfalls, instead of to Jesus. I had expected of her the perfection that only God could give me. Finally, though, I began to realize the depth of my sin. As I did, I learned not just to place my complete trust in Jesus, but also to believe that He is more than enough for me. I began to realize that Jesus is all I need to fill the emptiness and dissatisfaction of my life, and that only Jesus can bring the true fullness that I long for. Fullness will never come from your spouse. Don't expect from your spouse only what Jesus can fulfill because that's only setting your marriage up to fail as I learned the hard way.

Now I believe that if everything is taken away from me, but I have Jesus in my heart and mind, I have everything I need. As Jesus Himself reminded us in John 10:10, *"The thief comes only to steal and kill and destroy; I have come that they may have life, and have it to the full."* I could be in hell, but if I had Jesus, I would be okay. And even if I were in heaven, but if I did not have Jesus, I would have nothing and would truly be in hell.

First things first. We first need Jesus, and all of Jesus. What I mean is we need to abide by His teachings and commands. Our faith in His words is how we experience all of Him. If Jesus said it, then I believe and follow it. When we follow the order of Jesus first, our spouses second, and then our family, we will be filled. We don't need our spouse or family to try to lift the deepest burdens of our heart, for they can't.

What's more, when we give our burdens, desires and needs to Jesus, we receive full freedom and we are then ready to grace others— without expecting anything in return. Yes, we can use that noun as a verb. And "gracing" others is far better and more satisfying than waiting to be graced by others.

We must only look to Jesus for ultimate acceptance, and not to anyone else. If I am good with God and He is good with me, then I am approved by the one who created me and loves me more than anyone can. So either God is more than enough for me, or He is not. And the simple fact is that if God is enough for me, then I will be happy.

It's clear to me now: I've learned through godly counseling, to be love-focused and not need-focused, so I can focus on the number one commandment God gave us: to love God first, and then love others. Get it? Not ourselves, but others. When I place the needs of my spouse before my own, I find contentment in knowing that I am loving God by loving my spouse.

Scripture reminds us of the same thing. In Matthew 22: 37-39, Jesus told us to " *'Love the Lord your God with all your heart and with all your soul and with all your mind.' This is the first and greatest commandment. And the second is like it: 'Love your neighbor as yourself.' All the Law and the Prophets hang on these two commandments.* "

Yet somehow in marriage and in life, we forget to do this, and thus break God's number one command. Remember, though, that it is God who deserves our sacrifice of love. So if we love God first then we will display our love for Him by sacrificially loving others first, right? We can directly display our love for God, by loving others!

First, however, we need to get right with God and receive His grace for our countless sins. Why? Because unless we first understand our failures, how will we be able to forgive others who have failed us? To love God we must love others, and to love others, we need to forgive others. See what I'm trying to say? Are you a forgiving person, just as God forgives you?

Even if you are a great person in your eyes, think about this. When was the last time you spent a complete hour loving God 100 percent, each second? When was the last time you were so focused in your mind about God that you placed God first—without any distractions? When was the last time you then truly loved God, the way He asked us to?

If we're honest, we're all convicted on this count. We have all failed at this particular sin, let alone the others. Can you ask God to forgive you, so you can receive God's grace, in order to grace others who have wronged you? The one whose sins are the greatest, are the ones who can forgive the most. As Jesus told us, "*Therefore, I tell you, her many sins have been forgiven—for she loved much. But he who has been forgiven little loves little.*" (Luke 7:47)

I would rather love others, which is a far greater joy, than expect to be loved. As the apostle Paul told the Ephesian believers, "*In everything I did, I showed you that by this kind of hard work we must help the weak, remembering the words the Lord Jesus himself said: 'It is more blessed to give than to receive.'*" (Acts 20:35)

So I know I will always have a great day when my focus is on loving others. Try this: Love those who do not love you. You will be blessed. To love those who have hurt you is a blessing from God and can only be done through God's grace.

Who do you need to show grace to today?

CHAPTER 20

LOVING GOD, LOVING OTHERS, TRUSTING HIM

Jesus replied: " 'Love the Lord your God with all your heart and with all your soul and with all your mind.' This is the first and greatest commandment. And the second is like it: 'Love your neighbor as yourself.' All the Law and the Prophets hang on these two commandments."
(Matthew 22:37-40)

My CFO, Kevin Miller, sometimes has the unpleasant task of delivering not-so-good news. That was the case in 2009, a year during which my marriage was being restored... even as the economy and our business were still struggling.

Kevin was the one to remind me of rising business costs and declining sales. That was of course not a good combination, and the bad news showed on his face as he shared the unhappy numbers. If ever there was a time our business needed God's wisdom, it has been the last three years. So we have prayed and prayed and prayed for the Lord's direction and wisdom. And during these times of economic heartache, He has answered—only not in ways we always expect.

Here's an example from just a few years before, during a time when our wholesale company, *Not of This World,* was actually doing quite well at a well-known national retailer. As a matter of fact, *Not of This World* shirts were selling better than other brands in their stores. So obviously they were pleased with the performance, and we were happy to spread the gospel through our shirts.

Until one day we got an unexpected call from their buyer. The problem? Not that sales were poor. Not that we weren't living up to our agreements. What then?

Simply that our message was too strong. And because of that, their upper management had decided to remove *Not of This World* from their shelves. Just like that.

We were devastated. How could this happen? But out the door we went, losing a half-million dollar account. You can guess how that kind of loss affects a business. It hurts.

Except that God is in control now, just as he was then. And several months later we learned that the national retailer who had done so well with our *Not of This World* had just filed for chapter 11.

Once more we were amazed at God's grace. God had kept us from losing all of our money by removing us from their stores a year earlier. Do you see how God provides? We would have lost it all had God not removed us. He knew what He was doing, even if we didn't.

Meanwhile, according to every news report, 2009 was still going down as a financial disaster. I prayed relentlessly to God for His direction and rescue. If we were going to get through it, we needed God's help. But the more I focused on my troubles, the worse things appeared to be in my mind.

As the months passed, I began to accept that I had no control over the economy or its ill effects on our company. It was only by God's grace that I began focusing on Him and not on all the problems. Through the summer and into the fall, I was able to manage the business accordingly; the difference was that I didn't let all the problems get to me.

2009 was the year God taught me how He gives us peace and joy when our true focus is on loving Him first and loving others second, instead of focusing on the things we think we need. Remember what Jesus called the "first and greatest commandment"?

" *'Love the Lord your God with all your heart and with all your soul and with all your mind.' This is the first and greatest commandment. And the second is like it: 'Love your neighbor as yourself.' All the Law and the Prophets hang on these two commandments. "* (Matthew 22:37-40)

As believers we may be good about obeying the Great Commission of sharing the gospel, or at least talking about it. But the Great Commandment of Jesus is often overlooked. Still, I found that when I obeyed His Great Commandment fully, and focused on it, I could then trust Him to provide for my needs according to His abundant grace and perfect will.

This applied to my personal life, and to my business life. There was no difference. God used Dr. Bob Hughes and his great book *(Love Focused)* to teach me to focus on what really matters in life—and that's Him!

God wants us to focus on loving Him first, and we do this by loving others. Not by worrying, not by disagreeing with His decisions, but by trusting in Him and His sovereign ways. And if we focus on the great commandment of loving Him by loving others, then He loves us by providing for our needs. I applied this principle that difficult year. And to my surprise, instead of focusing on getting things accomplished the way I wanted them, I found I really could focus on just loving God. Reading His Word and acting like a child who is waiting for His father provided me the peace and joy that I needed.

In a very practical way, I learned in 2009 that when we accept God's provisions for us with thanksgiving and praise, we are freed from the cares of this world. Accepting God's all-sufficient grace allows us to be thankful to God for how things are—right now. Jesus didn't say "Think about yourself, get that now, take care of this, worry about that…"

He did, however, command us to love Him above all, and love others like ourselves.

It was so simple. Why didn't I get it before? We can either love God and love others, or we can pursue things which we have no control over. Either God was going to honor His word to take care of me, or He was not. But as I found out, God is really faithful, even when we are not. So we can try to exercise control over things and be disappointed time and time again, or we can choose to trust God's goodness and perfect will for our lives.

And I asked myself, *Which would you rather do?*

Scripture calls on us to *"Trust in the Lord with all your heart and lean not on your own understanding; in all your ways acknowledge him, and he will make your paths straight."* (Proverbs 3:5-6)

This verse again reminded me to not trust in what I knew about the world. When I think about how I tried to fix things my own way, well, it's no secret how badly I failed. But when I learned to finally trust Him, when I finally decided not to live with my fears, that's when I finally began winning... in the true sense of the word.

I have to admit that letting go of tough situations that were out of my control was difficult. There were a lot of dollars involved, for one thing. But by God's grace I have been able to do so by trial and error. If I realize that things are out of my hands, then they are out of my hands. Period. So how can I worry about things that are not in my hands? Get it? Do what you can, and then after that wait upon the Lord.

The one thing in life that I found to have control over was my ability to love God, to love others, and to trust God for His results and outcomes. It all came together, in that order.

So if we focus and obey God's Great Commandment—loving Him and loving others—we are then freed to trust God to provide for our needs. What a great freedom that is! When we realize that we don't have control (and really, we never have), then we're compelled to trust God, Who actually *is* in control.

So now what's your decision? It's up to you. What is God calling you trust Him fully in, right now? Can you say, "God is enough and that is more than okay with me"?

Here's another way to look at it, and a helpful self-test. I learned how harmful habits like fear, guilt, and worry were often the result of seeking to control and pursue selfish goals and desires. So were jealousy, pride, greed, lust, and anger... among other things. I grew up in a family where worrying was considered a virtue. It took me nearly 50 years to figure out who is in control.

Add to the list unbelief and doubt, as well. Whether it was just one, or more than one, these destructive habits actually served as warning signs that I was not fully seeking and trusting God. Since then, through a lot of practice, I've begun to recognize these warning signals. The good news is that we're free to leave these destructive habits behind, and this is the abundant life that Jesus came to give us.

So let's look at ourselves carefully and honestly. When we admit that we aren't in control of this world and its circumstances, and realize that God is our creator and actual provider, we can focus on loving God, by actually loving others.

Today, instead of worrying about my business challenges and walking around the office like the sky is falling, I make a conscious decision to love on people. Simple? Yes. Easy? No. But I ask God to help me in this area as well.

Looking back on the past few years, I can't count how many times I left the office exhausted because of my fears and doubts. But I thank God for the help and encouragement I received that year to better help me learn how to rest in God by completely trusting Him to provide whatever outcome He wants for us—and then to live at peace about it. The simple fact is that either God is enough for us or He is not. There are no in-betweens. And if God is enough, then nothing can be a threat.

Nothing.

When God is enough for you, then whatever trial you experience allows you to be at peace. This is true no matter how hard the trial may be. Take a look at what the Apostle Paul wrote to the believers in Philippi: *"Let your gentleness be evident to all. The Lord is near. Do not be anxious about anything, but in everything, by prayer and petition, with thanksgiving, present your requests to God. And the peace of God, which transcends all understanding, will guard your hearts and your minds in Christ Jesus."* (Philippians 4:5-7)

So if we understand and believe that the Lord is near (as this verse assures us) and we obey God's greatest commandment to love Him and love others (as Jesus Himself commands us), then God graciously provides for our needs.

Pause for a moment here to take inventory. Have you been struggling with any fears, doubts, or worry? Maybe the fact that you are reading this book is God's way of telling you that He loves you and He will provide for your needs no matter what. Will you choose to believe that God is good and He wants to bless you? Are there things in your life that you need to trust and wait on the Lord for right now? We can all think of something. But what does trusting God mean? To trust in the Lord means to wait and to be patient, and patience means longsuffering.

Can you trust and wait upon a known God for an unknown future? Can you thank the Lord for the way things are at this moment, however tough things may be? Here's reassurance from Scripture:

"...we also rejoice in our sufferings, because we know that suffering produces perseverance; perseverance, character; and character, hope. And hope does not disappoint us, because God has poured out his love into our hearts by the Holy Spirit, whom he has given us." (Romans 5:3-5)

God can either take your particular trial away quickly if He wants to, or He can give you the added grace you need to endure and persevere through your trials. No matter what option God chooses, it requires a conscious decision in your mind to accept whatever He wants for you in this particular season of your life. The key here is to remember that seasons don't last forever.

When we look at the second part of God's greatest commandment, the Lord clearly commands us to love our neighbor as ourselves. That much is obvious. But think about this: If we are required to love others as ourselves, we are also then required to forgive others first, right?

We can find plenty of instances in Scripture where we're called to forgive. Paul wrote to the church in Colossae that they should *"Bear with each other and forgive whatever grievances you may have against one another. Forgive as the Lord forgave you."* (Colossians 3:13)

In any relationship, before we can truly love, we must truly forgive. So how can we not forgive others who have wronged us when Jesus has already forgiven us? I faced that decision often in my business dealings with less-than-perfect people, less-than-perfect suppliers, and less-than-perfect criticism of our business. In each case, I had to ask, wasn't it our sins that crucified Jesus? Wasn't it *my* sins?

Believers need to recognize two major roadblocks to loving others. First, our pride can lead to an unloving attitude. Pride hinders us from loving others because our focus is on ourselves and not on others. Yet it can be hard to see in ourselves, and it happens more often than we think. I know this from personal experience. There have been far too many times where I have been wronged, and instead of forgiving the other person, I chose to stay angry just because it felt good to stay angry, in an awful sort of way. Can you relate to this?

I remember during a stressful season at work, I found myself practically disabled by continuous headaches. Before work, after work.... my head would not stop throbbing. Finally I went to the doctor for testing, only to be told there was nothing wrong with me.

Nothing wrong? Then why wouldn't the terrible headaches stop? The doctor could only tell me to try to reduce my stress on the job, and recommended a few pills. So I left the doctor's office still without answers until God dropped the real answer on me—right there in the car.

God revealed to me that my problem wasn't that I was too busy. Stress at work wasn't the main cause. There was only one real reason: I needed to forgive a certain person at work. And to my surprise, once I forgave him the next day, my headaches simply went away. Amazing!

Here's the second roadblock keeping us from loving others:

overwhelming feelings of guilt and condemnation over our sins. But let's be clear: Condemnation comes from Satan, and is very different than conviction. Conviction only comes from knowing Jesus and leads us to repent and return to God. It is actually God's grace leading us to return to Him. *"For the grace of God that brings salvation has appeared to all men. It teaches us to say 'No' to ungodliness and worldly passions…"* (Titus 2:11)

But it doesn't have to be that way. Paul wrote clearly that *"Therefore, there is now no condemnation for those who are in Christ Jesus…"* (Romans 8:1) No condemnation. None! Which part of this inspired Scripture do we not understand? There is a great freedom and peace knowing and believing we have been forgiven, no matter what we have done in our past. When we repent of our sins, turning away from them to the arms of Jesus, we are forgiven. It is final. That's why Jesus said *"It is finished"* as he was hanging on the cross. (See John 19:30.)

So if Jesus has already forgiven us completely by His atoning sacrifice on the cross, shouldn't we also forgive ourselves?

It takes a conscious decision. It takes faith in Jesus. But when we consciously forgive ourselves, we are in turn freed and empowered to fully love others in the power of Christ—without expecting those people to be or to act a certain way. It doesn't matter how many times we have been hurt, or how bad the offense was.

When we truly believe in our hearts that we have been forgiven, we can then love others. But what does that mean, exactly? Again Scripture tells us in the clearest terms: *"Love is patient, love is kind. It does not envy, it does not boast, it is not proud. It is not rude, it is not self-seeking, it is not easily angered, it keeps no record of wrongs. Love does not delight in evil but rejoices with the truth. It always protects, always trusts, always hopes, always perseveres."* (1 Corinthians 13:4-7)

I would like you to pause and take some time to be honest with yourself and with God. Please close your eyes right now and go before God in prayer, asking this question: Have I truly accepted God's forgiveness for all of my sins? All of them?

Accept the fact that even though God hates your sins, He loves you! Do you understand and agree with this great truth? Do you grasp the fact that it's not about how good you are, but about how good God is and what He did on the cross for us? *"Blessed is the man whose sin the LORD does not count against him and in whose spirit is no deceit."* (Psalms 32:2)

Have you accepted the way God has made you? Have you thanked Him for how He has made you? Even though you may not like yourself right now, God loves you, and you are special to Him. God created you and He loves just the way you are. Believe this and receive this. To Him you are perfectly and wonderfully made, and that's what matters.

"I praise you because I am fearfully and wonderfully made; your works are wonderful, I know that full well." (Psalm 139:14) Ask God to help you realize and believe in your heart that He loves you no matter how imperfect you may feel. God has made you in His image and you are forever special to Him.

I will say this again: God loves you 100 percent, not 98 percent. I emphasize this so that you may be sympathetic with other people who are struggling like yourself, and help them get close to God. Do you get this? You are not alone!

Allow God to fully wash all your sins and guilt away right now. Place them at the foot of the cross, walk away from them and into His abundant, never ending grace. Why? Because God wants the best for you, He loves you, and because Jesus paid for our past, present and future sins with His life. For all of the consequences of our sins, He paid for them all. All of them.

Now that I have shared what I have gleaned from God's Greatest Commandment, I want to show how God gave me perseverance to endure some of my toughest trials yet.

CHAPTER 21

NEVER GIVE UP!

...pursue righteousness, godliness, faith, love, endurance, and gentleness. Fight the good fight of the faith...
(1 Timothy 6:11-12)

In mid-2009, I was approached with an opportunity to acquire a flailing Christian clothing brand, *Truth Soul Armor.* We had carried *Truth Soul Armor* clothing in our C28 stores for years. I knew the original owners and now knew the president of the company, Jeff Ray. But we had reservations. At the time, it didn't make sense to invest money on another clothing brand when our business was struggling financially. Our *Not of This World* clothing brand was growing at the wholesale level, but our C28 retail stores were still in the red, month after month.

What to do? I prayed a lot over this decision and eventually God made it clear to me to go forward with it. How? The Lord placed a burden on my heart, a crystal clear conviction, to not allow this brand to go the direction of other brands that had lost their Christian bearings. It disappointed me to see some of those Christian companies move away from their original, faith-filled starting points. I just didn't want that to happen to *Truth Soul Armor.*

One thing that helped me through the complexity and stress of acquiring another company was the wisdom of an army officer friend named Richard. Knowing where he stood with the Lord, I hoped he could offer me something deep, something spiritual. Something to help me in this decision.

Instead Richard looked at me and jabbed at the air with his finger. "Never give up," he told me. "Never! Fight the good fight until the finish." Well, it's pretty hard to ignore or forget that kind of advice. *Persevere!*

Perseverance means to never give up despite any obstacles that may come our way. Talent, education, or even money will not help us reach ultimate success. But perseverance and hard work, fueled and sustained by faith in Jesus, will. Richard's words still rang in my ears as I continued to pray for wisdom.

As you now know, I have experienced many wins as well as many losses. And by God's grace I have been able to persevere through the trials of life—not by my own abilities, but only by relying on God's power and His grace. And this is for you as well!

One great secret is that through daily Bible reading and prayer, I have experienced God to be abundantly faithful. He has always given me that extra measure of grace I needed to persevere, and to thrive. He is always more than generous.

I've found that perseverance brings victories, and victories are always around the corner. Just as we are about to give up, victory through the Lord is near! Did you know that Walt Disney went bankrupt three times before starting Disneyland? Disney never gave up.

As I write this in 2010, the economy is still tough. We're still looking for a recovery. After three of the most difficult years ever, I feel as if we are only halfway through this tunnel. Yet I persevere and look to Jesus, my Sustainer. As the apostle Paul reminded Christians in the city of Corinth, *"We are hard pressed on every side, but not crushed; perplexed, but not in despair; persecuted, but not abandoned; struck down, but not destroyed."* (2 Corinthians 4:8-9) I love to meditate on this Scripture.

I've had my share of struggles and defeats, but I know that I'm not alone. I know many of you reading this have also experienced difficult times but know that God has a purpose behind the trials we all face.

Trials and defeats are often God's tools of His love, and they're actually required in order to grow one's faith and trust in God. *"… For he will be like a refiner's fire or a launderer's soap. He will sit as a refiner and purifier of silver; he will purify the Levites and refine them like gold and silver…"* (Malachi 3:2-3) When God loves us, He often refines us because we are special to Him. So when the Lord is refining us, stop and realize it is He who is doing the work in you, and then allow Him to complete the work. After the trial is over, you will be blessed. Believe me, this is true!

So there is a purpose for perseverance, and we can be encouraged by the Scripture which reminds us how *"Perseverance must finish its work so that you may be mature and complete, not lacking anything."* (James 1:4)

What's more, without trials in our lives, we wouldn't experience the sweet victories. The book of James has much to say about this, as well as about perseverance. Again we read that *"…we consider blessed those who have persevered. You have heard of Job's perseverance and have seen what the Lord finally brought about. The Lord is full of compassion and mercy."* (James 5:11)

Here are a few points I've learned from reading God's Word on perseverance:

Perseverance brings restoration. Even though I do not know *when* or *how* God is going to fix things, I just *know* that God will help me. I know that He will restore things because I have His promises in writing. God is so clear when He tells us, *"So do not throw away your confidence; it will be richly rewarded. You need to persevere so that when you have done the will of God, you will receive what He has promised."* (Hebrews 10:35-36)

Perseverance brings comfort. I pray that you will not give up, so that you may experience the kind of perseverance Scripture describes. I pray you will come to realize that your relationship with Jesus and His grace is more than enough for you, no matter how difficult your situation and no matter how long you've been waiting for relief. During my most trying times of waiting on God, I've often turned to the comforting words of Psalm 13, written by King David. It's quite short—only six verses—and I have read and prayed this Scripture often.

"How long, O Lord? Will you forget me forever? How long will you hide your face from me? How long must I wrestle with my thoughts and every day have sorrow in my heart? How long will my enemy triumph over me? Look on me and answer, O Lord my God. Give light to my eyes, or I will sleep in death; my enemy will say, 'I have overcome him,' and my foes will rejoice when I fall. But I trust in your unfailing love; my heart rejoices in your salvation. I will sing to the Lord, for he has been good to me." (Psalm 13)

In prayer, you can also claim this psalm as yours right now. Go ahead—read and pray these verses to yourself out loud. Read them over and don't be shy to repeat them. Let the words become your words, and your prayer. The Lord will comfort you when you choose to believe in Him and His holy words.

If your faith is in Jesus, then you can rest assured that in spite of your present difficulties, whatever they may be, God will never leave you nor forsake you. Jesus promises that *"...surely I am with you always, to the very end of the age."* (Matthew 28:20) It's very clear. He has promised to be with us to the end. You may not fully understand or appreciate your current challenges, and you may never learn the reason why you're going through what you're going through. But never forget that God is here, and He is in control. God loves you!

If your problem is sin (and God will show you that if you ask Him), then repent and confess your sins to Him right now. He will forgive you. God will never give up on you, no matter how many times you have messed up. Persevere in faith, trusting that whatever difficulty you are going through, God truly knows what is best for you.

Remember this verse that I've referred to earlier: *"When times are good, be happy; but when times are bad, consider: God has made the one as well as the other..."* Ecclesiastes 7:14) Seasons change, and so will your circumstances. Rejoice in whatever season God has you going through. Rejoice. Ask God to use your struggles so that one day you will use them as a testimony to His goodness and bless others.

Never give up, remembering that failure is not falling down, but staying down. Whether you feel as if you're in want or in plenty, thank God right now, knowing that God truly loves you.

God loves to restore broken relationships, marriages, families, businesses—and even our health. God will either take away your trials, or God will give you the needed grace to endure and persevere. Either way, freedom will come to you when you consciously surrender your circumstances over to Him... daily. Make a deliberate choice today to trust and believe that God is more than enough in your life.

I will say it again, as my friend Richard reminded me: Never give up, because God really loves you! May *"The LORD bless you and keep you; the LORD make his face shine upon you and be gracious to you; the LORD turn his face toward you and give you peace."* (Numbers 6:24-26)

CHAPTER 22

DON'T DOUBT, JUST BELIEVE!

*The thief comes only to steal and kill and destroy; I have come
that they may have life, and have it to the full.*
(John 10:10)

That night a crowd of thousands packed into the open-air public mall where we'd scheduled the C28 outreach concert. The kids were loud and excited, and seemed to appreciate the music. I gave my testimony, as I often did to groups across the country. But then Joseph Rojas, the lead singer from Seventh Day Slumber (a popular Christian rock band) really got their attention.

How many of the crowd had thought about suicide, he asked… *that day?* And how many had actually written a letter to kill themselves… *that night?*

It seemed like a long shot, though in the past we had sometimes asked how many kids had ever thought about suicide. In the past, thousands had raised their hands. We knew it was a huge issue. Even more had raised their hands when we had specifically asked how many had considered suicide in the past month.

But this time Joseph faced them squarely with his penetrating, personal question. I really wasn't sure what would happen. But to my surprise, 14 kids raised their hands! And all 14 came forward to dedicate their lives to Christ.

From death to life. Amazing grace! But God wasn't finished, yet. Because not long after that a very large man also came forward, and he was weeping. As it turned out, his son was one of the 14 kids who had come forward, and who had been given new life in Jesus Christ.

Does it get any better? Shortly after coming to Christ I prayed that God would use whatever gifts and talents He had given me for His glory. I prayed that God would allow me to share the gospel through my testimony in front of thousands.

In response, the Lord opened doors for me to speak at countless schools, both private and public, from elementary to college. He has brought me to places where others have not wanted to go. Places where I had to pray for extra safety to get home. I have spoken at special events, churches, businesses, and outreaches. To kindergarteners and teenagers, old people, businessmen, and prisoners.

I have shared my testimony in front of thousands of people, and thousands have responded to the call of Christ. And I have driven to places 300 miles each way, or flown across the country, only to see a dozen people show up. But I would do it all over again if one person would come to Christ. Because no matter where I go, everyone in the audience has one thing in common: They all need Jesus!

I must confess that in the early years I had shared my testimony so often—sometimes several times a week—that I began to get tired of doing it. So I asked a pastor friend of mine, Steve Wilburn, how he kept from not growing weary of sharing the gospel so often. Steve looked at me and said, "Preach the gospel like it is your very last time." That advice has stayed with me. So I share my testimony anywhere, any place, whenever God wants me to go. I always say "yes!" if I possibly can.

Yet even with all of this awesome work taking place around me, and God's Holy Spirit showing me new things all the time, I can still doubt how God could truly use a wretch like me in ministry. In fact, one of my greatest struggles has been unbelief, which has often robbed me of the peace and joy I desire. At times I wondered if God was somehow angry at me. Look at how extremely difficult it was for C28 and *Not of This World,* year after year.

Never mind that. I suppose I could have chosen to do many other things besides this business. Perhaps I would have made millions. But I never would have witnessed tens of thousands coming to Christ.

Having said this, and even though God uses me to reach the lost, I still worry sometimes that He is done with me. Oh, if I could just believe 100 percent of what I already know to be true about God, my life would be more abundant. It's easy to write this book, but it's so much more difficult to do what I say.

Unfortunately, unbelief is a common problem. And unfortunately we all suffer to some degree from the consequences of doubt in our lives. In my case, I have often wondered how many opportunities God has given me over the years. But since opportunities usually come disguised as problems, I have often run away from them, and thus missed the blessings God had for me.

From time to time I've experienced worries, fears, jealousy, doubts, anxieties… the list goes on. They drive me away from the joy God has for me in the trials of life. If I could only believe in Him, rather than in my unpredictable, ever-changing circumstances, life would be much simpler.

I remember how much I feared losing Dogloo, the company that I spent my entire young adult life building. But all the while God had something way better for me. I remember doubting God in the early years of C28, as I questioned if God was truly involved in all the details. Did I need to worry? As I have stated previously, thousands of people have come to faith in Christ through the ministry of C28.

I remember doubting if C28 stores and NOTW would ever break even, but that was before we had six consecutive profitable years. I look back at both stock market crashes (2001 and 2008), and the plunge in my real estate values. I thought I would end up broke and destitute, but God took care of me financially. I doubted that God would bring Peggy and me back together, but God has restored our marriage to a wonderful place it's never been before. All this to say… do not worry, fear, or doubt. God is way bigger than our problems. With Jesus as my Lord and Savior, I leaned on Him to get me through all my trials. He never abandoned me.

I've learned that unbelief is one of Satan's tools to distract me away from God and steal my joy in the Lord Jesus. Doubts and thoughts of unbelief blind me from the fact that God is good and always loves His people—no matter what! So I remind myself that Satan is the great accuser and my enemy: *"The thief comes only to steal and kill and destroy; I have come that they may have life, and have it to the full."* (John 10:10)

God offers me an abundant, thriving life through a relationship with Jesus. By my faith in Him, He has bought my soul with His life, and therefore He wants all good things for me. It sounds too good to be true. But He really has, and He really does!

I rest in the fact that I am just a work in progress and God is not done with me until I die. Even when my faith is weak, He is strong—strong enough to make me what I cannot be without Him. Jesus said, *"The work of God is this: to believe in the one he has sent."* (John 6:29) So I am encouraged to know that even though God sees my weaknesses, He encourages me to confess the sins of unbelief and doubt to Him. Even if my belief is weak, God can take the little faith I have and multiply it. He loves to do this!

So… *"Let us then approach the throne of grace with confidence, so that we may receive mercy and find grace to help us in our time of need."* (Hebrews 4:16) I have felt and acted like a hypocrite often, but the words of Jesus help me to overcome my faults. I don't want to allow Satan to convince me that I am the biggest hypocrite alive. Look at what the apostle Paul said about himself: *"I know that nothing good lives in me, that is, in my sinful nature. For I have the desire to do what is good, but I cannot carry it out... Who will rescue me from this body of death?"* (Romans 7:18, 24b)

Without a shadow of a doubt, I can always approach the throne of grace to get right with God. Here's how it works. If you mess up (the way I do), confess it to God and begin to obey Him again. He is your Father and He will help you. And when we receive God's Word into our hearts and obey Jesus, we demonstrate that we are God's children.

The world screams at us to obey our feelings and desires (to be self-centered), and to do the things that temporarily feel good to our flesh. Christ teaches us the opposite. For example, if I had obeyed my feelings about C28 in the beginning, I would have closed the business and moved on without seeing the huge blessings that have followed. If I had obeyed my feelings when my marriage was on the rocks, I would have divorced my wife and missed the Lord's amazing blessing in our marriage. Get it? Don't follow feelings, but follow Jesus and His words.

I can either choose to be eternally focused or temporally focused. I can choose to be happy that my future is secure in Christ alone, or I can choose to follow my desires and flesh—which will eventually lead to my destruction. I've noticed how the pleasures of sin never last, but how the aftermath of sin can last forever. Sin destroys. Sin hurts others. That's why I strive to obey God's commands, with a focus on eternity. And God willing, the result will be that other people will know I am His. *"Those who obey his commands live in him, and he in them. And this is how we know that he lives in us..."* (1 John 3:24)

Speaking of obedience, it was when I finally surrendered C28 to God that He graciously blessed and multiplied the business. God has grown C28 Christian retail stores to 10 retail locations, an ecommerce site (www.c28.com), and four in-house clothing brands: NOTW, *Truth Soul Armor, Canvas,* and *Edify.* God has also blessed C28 with a non-profit outreach ministry (www.C28outreach.com) through which I am able to share my testimony and preach the gospel all over the country.

So it doesn't matter what doubts we may have about God. The fact is that if we believe in Jesus, we are righteous by faith alone. Don't be discouraged to learn you are far from perfect. God already knows this and still loves us. God anticipates that we'll fail, but He does not expect us to live in our failures. Leave your mistakes behind you and strive to obey Him in the power of the Holy Spirit, believing that Jesus does what you cannot.

I must admit it can sometimes be a little surreal to believe these amazing truths. But by God's grace and the help of the Holy Spirit we can receive His truths, and believe in them. So the question is, Will you believe in everything Jesus has shown us?

Will you choose to believe in His amazing grace and His power to enable you to do the impossible?

CHAPTER 23

FOREVER HIS!

*Never will I leave you; never will I forsake you. So we say with
confidence, "The Lord is my helper; I will not be afraid.
What can man do to me?"*
(Hebrews 13:5b-6)

Years ago, one of our first hires at C28 was Sarah, who started as a young sales clerk at our very first store at the Tyler mall in Riverside, California. And it wasn't long before we knew we had made a very good choice. As my sister Sonia trained her, it soon became very clear what a hard worker Sarah was.

As time went on Sarah grew as an employee; she eventually stepped up to become our first C28 district manager. But there was much more to Sarah than just professional skill. More importantly, Sarah was a prayer warrior, and she would encourage everyone around her to pray, as well.

As she did so, Sarah also did an awesome job of motivating her staff, as well as all of us at the corporate office. For anyone who was lonely or just going through a tough time, she would say things like, "Don't believe the lies of the enemy—just pray!" And she demonstrated that truth with her life. So whenever we needed a little encouragement, Sarah was always there to pray with us. And if God was not talking to Sarah, she would simply start talking to God in praise. Sarah had a gift to believe with a child-like faith. She would encourage others to pray right now for God's peace. And the thing is He always did it when asked!

I learned that lesson over the first decade, since we opened the first C28 store. Pray. Believe. Praise. These have been the best 10 years of my life, and getting to know the Lord through the ministry of C28 has been extremely rewarding. How could it not be? Having a front lines ministry in public places like malls has been extremely productive for the gospel. Countless lives have been eternally changed through God's Holy Spirit, and we praise God. Our company mission is to share the life-changing gospel message of grace and truth in Jesus Christ.

But here's the thing: Despite all the good news, I've experienced a personal battle by comparing these days to the profitable Dogloo years. I've even asked God, "Was C28 your idea, or mine? How long will we struggle with the finances?" But really, I already know the answer. Because C28 was birthed through prayer, that's how I know it was His idea, and it's all about God.

I know that God granted me early financial success (with Dogloo) to enable me to enter my faith walk. And while I know this for a fact, I must admit that as a business person, I have often fought the desires to have the kind of financial success I once enjoyed, years ago. I do not want to look back, but I wonder sometimes.

It's a little like that story in the Old Testament, when Abraham's nephew Lot and his wife fled Sodom and Gomorrah as the city burned. Lot's wife made one crucial mistake: She disobeyed God's command to not look back as they departed the city or else He would turn them into a pillar of salt. Unfortunately, Lot's wife did look back and suffered the consequence. I ask the Lord to help me so I never look back. I want to only look forward to Him!

In spite of our many sins and faults of looking back, God has been faithful. He has given us six profitable years in the first 10 years of business. I cannot complain. Honestly, when I think about what I deserve because of my sinful nature, it is easy for me to realize how fortunate I truly am. I am blessed beyond imagination, a graced man indeed.

Do I ever doubt? Yes, of course. Who doesn't? But whenever I have doubts in my mind about how we are doing financially, God always reminds me that He has not forgotten me. He reminds me that it was His idea and that He will prosper us and help us at the right time to allow us to keep reaching people with His love and grace.

We all have dreams and aspirations, and we all regret mistakes we've made along the way. At times we may all feel as if God is not paying attention to us, as if God has abandoned us in a tough economy. We may feel as if we have wronged Him and He is done with us. Or we know the disappointment of dreams that haven't yet come true.

But in all this, please always remember that God's ways are greater and higher than our ways. So please let me leave you with just a few assurances of the Lord's powerful grace. It is by God's grace that He keeps us and blesses us. Even though we fail, even though we are less than perfect, we belong to Jesus and He takes care of our needs if we have placed our faith and trust in Him. If we believe in Him, then we are His forever.

So in the end it's not important what I think about myself; it only matters what God thinks about me. While at times I may not feel like God loves me, the fact is that He does. So God will always go out of His way to protect me when I depend on Him. I check my perspective by asking myself, "Am I truly depending on God's power to make things right, or am I depending on my own strength?"

And about fear... I have learned that fear of the unknown future never really helps me. Rather, faith in His promises gives me the hope to go on. While it may feel like God has left us, He never does. King David knew that feeling when he wrote: *"To you, O LORD, I called; to the Lord I cried for mercy: 'What gain is there in my destruction, in my going down into the pit? Will the dust praise you? Will it proclaim your faithfulness? Hear, O LORD, and be merciful to me; O LORD, be my help.'"* (Psalm 30:8-10)

David knew firsthand who had the power to save him, and he ran to God for His protection and peace. David's relationship with

God came alive as he called and waited upon the Lord in joyful expectation. And while David was far from perfect, he called on the One who always helped Him.

Know this and never forget: If you have placed your faith and trust in Jesus, God will keep you and protect you… no matter what! If you are like me and you sometimes feel that you are terrible and hopeless, get over it. In all honesty, you are probably worse than what you think, but God still loves you just the way you are.

Now about dry seasons… Maybe you are a longtime believer and you are going through those times when you do not hear God at all. I have gone through dry periods, as well, times where I feel so disconnected from God—even to the point of wondering if I'm even saved. This has happened more often than I would like to admit. And those doubts and accusations? Lies from the pit of hell. We know that Satan is the king of doubts and lies, and he loves to condemn us. By doing so, he can push us further away from God.

How can we act as if we are condemned when we believe in Jesus? Do we forget that *"Therefore, there is now no condemnation for those who are in Christ Jesus, because through Christ Jesus the law of the Spirit of life set me free from the law of sin and death"?* (Romans 8:1-2)

Whenever you are accused over and over again in your mind, I have found these are the best times to quickly run to the foot of the cross. That means admitting and confessing my sins to God, and leaving them with Jesus. It also means acknowledging the fact that Jesus paid the full price for my sins. All of them—my past, present and even future sins are left at the foot of the cross.

Have you done this? Have you placed your sins at the foot of the cross and left them there? If not, then I beg you to do so right now!

Get up, leave your sins behind you and look to Jesus. Let's learn to walk in faith, not by those misleading feelings.

It's an ongoing thing. Because even though I know God's truth and I believe that Jesus is my Lord and my Savior, the struggles and circumstances of this world can so quickly rob me of the assurances of God's reality and His everlasting love for me. But that's why we need to... *"Trust in the LORD with all your heart and lean not on your own understanding; in all your ways acknowledge him, and he will make your paths straight."* (Proverbs 3:5-6)

Of course, I can get so distracted. Remember back a few chapters when I described the struggles in my marriage, and how I thought my world was falling apart? I was not trusting God to repair my marriage at that moment. All I could see were the temporary problems around me. The more I focused on my problems instead of His promises, the more depressed I got. But thanks to God, He did restore my marriage. God is so faithful, especially when we are not. We do not have to know when or know how God will fix things; we just have to believe that He will!

As you already know, I'm not into rituals, but one daily practice that has helped me over the years is to spend time with God in prayer and reading His Holy Word each morning. When I spend time with God, His Word and His Holy Spirit reassure me that He is my father, and that I am His child—no matter how far I have drifted from Him or how many times I have messed things up. God will never leave me—ever! After all, Jesus said, *"I give them eternal life, and they shall never perish; no one can snatch them out of my hand. My Father, who has given them to me, is greater than all; no one can snatch them out of my Father's hand. I and the Father are one."* (John 10:28-30)

With this truth in mind, I can rest easy knowing that God never stops the work He has already begun in me, slow as it may seem. By reading God's Word, and meditating on it, I can often hear God's small voice through His Holy Spirit that keeps me close to Him. It says in the book of Proverbs, *"Keep my commands and you will live; guard my teachings as the apple of your eye. Bind them on your fingers; write them on the tablet of your heart."* (Proverbs 7:2-3)

Even after saying all this, though, and while I have known the Lord for over a decade, there are times when I feel as if I've made very little progress in my Christian walk. Sometimes I even feel as if I'm slipping backwards. I must admit that coming to Christ later in life has given me a lot of baggage that Satan often uses to condemn me, or to give me reasons and justification in my mind for continuing in my old bad habits, my old ways.

I know in this book I speak a lot about our sinful nature, but I have to remind myself that my new identity is in Christ. Who I am today in Christ is holy and blameless (Ephesians 1:4). When Jesus looks at me He looks at me through His eyes. And right there is the power of God to change my old destructive patterns through this truth of Scripture.

When people hurt me or say things about me that are not the truth, in my old ways (before I knew Christ), I feel like it is my right to defend myself. But in the process of making things right for myself, I end up obeying my old ways which produces anger, sarcasm, lust, greed, worry, fear and a host of other sins. How often do we say to ourselves, "That's just the way I am", or "That's what I always do", to justify wrong and destructive behaviors?

But here is the key: when I surrender my old sinful desires and look to Christ for His help, I see my identity is in Christ. I am a new creation in Christ Jesus (2Corinthians 5:17). I do not have to defend myself or free myself from old sinful patterns when I have Christ to do it for me. I make a conscious decision to believe in what Christ says in Romans 6:8-12. I don't believe the lies in my mind, but I choose to believe who I am in Jesus. I am now dead to sin and alive in Christ. By believing in my new identity, I'm not hostage to my past sinful desires anymore! And the icing on the cake is that God's Word reassures me of His love and continued faithfulness, especially when I confess my shortfalls to Him: *"being confident of this, that he who began a good work in you will carry it on to completion until the day of Christ Jesus."* (Philippians 1:6)

And I urge you, as you read the Bible, please don't just read it intellectually, the way you would a magazine or a textbook or a newspaper. Instead pray and ask the Holy Spirit to guide you into a deeper understanding of His messages for you. Look and search through it like gold, because God's secrets are often hidden deep within His writings. True seekers of God who read the Bible find life, comfort, joy and all good things from Him.

Never forget that when we belong to Jesus, sinful as we are, He treasures us as His greatest possession. He will keep us. He promises that *"Never will I leave you; never will I forsake you."* (Hebrews 13:5b) So because of faith in Jesus, little as it may seem at times, our future is an eternity with Him!

God loves you.

Author's note

I hope you enjoyed reading my journey from being an immigrant, to a businessman, to a follower of God. He is my passion and I pray that He becomes yours as well.

I wrote this book to change lives for the sake of Jesus Christ. And if there is just one thing I want you to take away from reading this book, it would be to know Jesus Christ as your Lord and Savior and to grow in a thriving relationship with Him. If this book has touched your life, please let me know by emailing me at testimony@c28.com. I encourage you to also read the next sections for resources and an important message from God.

All proceeds from this book are donated to C28 Outreach Ministry which is a nonprofit corporation designed to reach as many people as possible with the gospel of Jesus Christ through outreach concerts, speaking events, Bible distribution, and more. Please visit www.C28outreach.com to find out more or if you would like to get involved.

Jesus Loves You!

APPENDIX A:

Salvation message

Why we need Jesus...

If you're not sure where you're going when you die, and if you've felt a nudge on your heart while reading this book, be aware of one thing: God's Holy Spirit is knocking. It's because the One who created you and loves you is calling you to a brand-new life in Jesus. God knows you by name! Are you going to open the door to His love? Here's how it works...

1—What does it mean?

You must first understand how much God loves us. Know that He has plans for us and wants a close relationship with us. That's why we're on this planet. That's why we were born.

Do you already have some ideas about getting to know God? That shows you've been thinking. But the Holy Bible tells us we need Jesus. Without Him there is no access to God, no salvation, and no real purpose or peace in life.

Why do we need Jesus? Because the Holy Bible—which is the Word of God—calls us to be perfect as God is perfect. Instead we all fall short of that. Whether you have ever lied or killed, sin is sin. It's all the same to God. So when we die, each one of us will stand before God on judgment day. Unfortunately, the penalty of any sin is eternal hell, which means total separation from God for eternity—to burn in the Lake of Fire forever. It doesn't get any worse than that.

2—How does God grade?

The first basic question to answer is, are you a sinner? Ah, you don't like that word, huh? Okay, maybe you're not as bad as the next guy. You have done more good than bad, right? You're not a mass murderer, and you hardly ever get a parking ticket. You're doing okay, if God grades on a curve The problem is, He does not. Have you ever taken anything that doesn't belong to you? Have you ever stretched the truth? Ever hated anyone? If you answered "yes" to any of these questions (or even "well... maybe"), you've already broken one of the Ten Commandments. And that's just for starters—there are still seven more commandments to measure ourselves against.

3—Can't earn it, can't buy it

By now you must be thinking it's not looking so good. No one's perfect, right? Right. The Bible says that *"If we claim to be without sin, we deceive ourselves and the truth is not in us."* (1 John 1:8)

The Bible also teaches that if you break any of the Ten Commandments, then the penalty is judgment (death in hell). *"For the wages of sin is death..."* (Romans 6:23a)

Does that mean all of us—even your nice neighbor, your sweet grandma and you yourself—will be judged when we die? I'm afraid so. And if you're trying to be a good, moral and law-abiding citizen; someone who's trying to do good works and work your way into heaven... well, sorry; none of that measures up before a Holy God. Good moral people do go to hell every day.

That's the bad news. We're all sinners, and we have it coming. If you still can't buy that, you're stuck in reverse, and that is pride. Pride is at the root of every sin. God only deals with people who are willing to take off their rose-colored glasses and see life as it really is. When we finally admit we can't save ourselves, and we realize we need a Savior, we can call on Jesus for His help, and He will redeem us. So yes, there's some major good news. There is a way out of this mess. God does provide us with an awesome solution, but He does give us free will to choose it!

4—Our freedom

How do we escape judgment? God made a one-time substitution. Instead of *us* dying, Jesus (God in human flesh) died in our place taking the full wrath of God that we as humans deserve for our sins. This is called grace, and it's the only thing that works. Here's what the Bible says about that: *"For it is by grace you have been saved, through faith--and this not from yourselves, it is the gift of God—not by works, so that no one can boast."* (Ephesians 2:8-9)

Grace happened on the cross, once and for all. This human sacrifice covers our past, present and future sins. There is a better way to understand it. The Bible tells us, *"But he was pierced for our transgressions, he was crushed for our iniquities; the punishment that brought us peace was upon him, and by his wounds we are healed."* (Isaiah 53:5) Everyone who believes in Jesus and what He did is saved by His atoning sacrifice!

That's right—Jesus died for us, and more than that, he rose from the dead to prove God was in full control of the situation. It wasn't just for show; there's a plan behind His sacrifice.

5—Sealing the deal

The crucifixion is actually a gift…and what a gift! But like all gifts, the Giver needs a receiver. If we do not receive, if we choose not to believe or if we refuse His gift—then His sacrifice was in vain. And then we're back to square one: hell-bound, where we really don't want to be. By not choosing Jesus, you automatically choose hell. Read God's message in a nutshell:

"For God so loved the world that he gave his one and only Son, that whoever believes in him shall not perish but have eternal life. For God did not send his Son into the world to condemn the world, but to save the world through him. Whoever believes in him is not condemned, but whoever does not believe stands condemned already because he has not

believed in the name of God's one and only Son." (John 3:16-18)

So here's the plan. Forget trying to be perfect; you'll never make it and it's already too late for that, anyway. Just come as you are. When we repent and turn away from our sins, believe in Him, and accept Jesus Christ as Lord and Savior, we're saved.

"Lord and Savior." A lot of Christians say it like one word, "Lord-and-Savior." But there is really more to it. On the one hand, "Lord" is the president, prime minister, king, ruler and CEO rolled into one. He's the One we report to in everything, and I do mean *everything*. And the Scriptures confirm that Jesus is God. On the other hand, "Savior" is simply the One who saves us from the pit of hell. Get it?

6—Warning: Changes Ahead

Being saved, though, is a life-changing experience. We have to totally let go of control of our lives. The Bible calls it being "born again." You can verify this phrase in John chapter 3. When we're born again, we're filled with His Holy Spirit forever. That's good news for today, good news for tomorrow, good news…forever!

Remember, this is God's only solution, God's only provision. All roads do not lead to heaven, no matter how much we would wish it were true. The Bible clearly teaches that apart from Christ, there's no forgiveness of sin, no eternal life. There is no other door. This is it. *"Jesus answered, 'I am the way and the truth and the life. No one comes to the Father except through me.' "* (John 14:6)

Now, if you don't know Jesus, please don't close this book without taking a close look at what He's offering. Please. Because if you walk away, you're denying God and His love for you, and you may not ever get another opportunity. And if you're ready to go through with this, check out the next section for how to put God's plan into action.

APPENDIX B:

A life-changing prayer

Do you want to know the meaning of life? Why you were born? Are you wondering about going to heaven? Then, if you've never dedicated your heart and life to Jesus before, sincerely pray this life changing prayer below:

God in heaven, I come to you asking for your forgiveness of my sins, because I know I've sinned. I want to turn away from those sins. I also confess right now and believe with my heart that Jesus is God the Son, and that He died on the cross for me and rose from the dead so I may be forgiven of my sins and have eternal life. Jesus, please come into my life right now to be my Savior and Lord. From this day on, I will follow you. I place my faith and trust in you Jesus, not in the things of this world. And now I thank You, Father, for saving me. I believe your promises and thank you that I am born again; that I'm clean now because of what you've done for me in Jesus. Amen

You can be assured of your salvation if you prayed this prayer and meant it! Once you've done that, you can know that you're right with God, because *"...Everyone who calls on the name of the Lord will be saved."* (Romans 10:13)

If you already know Jesus, use this as a handy guide to share with others. If you don't know Jesus, this is for you. Either way, here's a brief, nine-step summary:

1. We have all sinned. Whether it's a lie or murder, sin is sin and the penalty is the same.

2. At death, we will all be judged. We will all have to give an account to God for our sins.

3. The penalty of sin is eternal hell. Hell is also called the "Lake

of Fire," and it's our due penalty, forever.

4. God provides us with a solution to our sin problem and penalty. God's Son Jesus died on a cross.

5. The solution is *Jesus*. God requires payment for sin to be paid with innocent, pure blood. Only Jesus' blood is acceptable to God as payment for mankind's sins because Jesus is God! His sacrifice became our payment for sin.

6. Through faith in Jesus, all of our sins (past, present and future) are washed away forever and we can spend eternity with Him.

7. Why does God do this? Because God loves us, is merciful and grants us grace through Jesus. He created us for Him.

8. How do I get saved? We turn from our sins and our old way of doing things and place our total faith and trust in Jesus. We move from a self-centered way of life to a God-centered way of life.

9. When does salvation happen? Immediately! Your soul is *permanently* sealed by the Holy Spirit.

Congratulations! Your new life will not be perfect, but when trials come, you will have Jesus to help you through them. Here are a few Bible verses to help you start your faith journey with God...

You're saved. You can be certain you're saved, that you're right with God. No one and nothing can take that away from you. So go ahead and rest in Jesus because your soul has been sealed by the Holy Spirit, forever! *"...God has given us eternal life, and this life is in his Son. He who has the Son has life; he who does not have the Son of God does not have life."* (1 John 5:11-12)

You're forgiven. From now on if you ask for His day-to-day forgiveness, He will forgive you right away. What's more, Jesus will work with you so you'll want to sin less and less. Remember, this verse is written for Christians, those who follow Jesus. *"If we confess our sins, he is faithful and just and will forgive us our sins* *and purify us from all unrighteousness."* (1 John 1:9)

You're never alone. And you can count on this promise: *"Never will I leave you; never will I forsake you."* (Hebrews 13:5b)

You've got a friend. If you have accepted Jesus Christ as Savior and Lord through the reading of this book and the leading of the Holy Spirit, would you please let me know? Just email me at testimony@ c28.com and we will send you free information to help you in your new walk with the Lord Jesus.

APPENDIX C:

Moving on; the Christian Life

It took me a few years after I first gave my life to Jesus before I started to understand, really grasp what the gospel was all about. I learned how the initial life-changing gospel message of Jesus Christ was also powerful for everyday living, for a fuller life today. But it took a while for me to see.

1—The Gospel of Grace

I didn't understand the gospel of grace right away. In fact, a few years after I came to Christ, I didn't feel close to God on account of my present sins. Yes, I'd been saved from paying the penalty of death, and I'd received mercy and grace instead. But I knew I still sinned, and that made me wonder: Did I really deserve God's love or attention?

That's when the power of the gospel began to change my life yet again, this time for everyday living. Bible truth was coming alive for me at Cornerstone Fellowship Bible Church in Riverside. Under the teaching of Pastor Milton Vincent, I started to recognize my ugly sinful nature more and more. But in the process the beautiful grace of Jesus grew more and more evident.

So I learned to appreciate God's mercy and savor His grace every day. It's like the closer I got to God, the dirtier I realized I was, and then the more I could appreciate God's awesome mercy and grace in Jesus. It's all connected.

Once I saw that truth, I would no longer be gripped, condemned and frozen out of commission by the guilt of my sins. I finally understood the grace I received through Jesus was 100 percent good not just for my past, but also my present and future sins. Yes, grace trumps sin! Paul the apostle talks about this in Romans chapters seven and eight. Paul himself knew what was right, and wanted to do right, but in his flesh he would do wrong. Yet he praised God because he found no condemnation in Christ Jesus.

However, this abundant grace does not give us a green light or license to sin. While we have the forgiveness of our daily sins through Jesus, we still have to face the consequences of our sins. So we don't want to distance ourselves from His blessings and we certainly don't want to grieve the very same Holy Spirit, that sealed our souls, by sinning. Check out Ephesians 4:30 for more about this.

In the end, the more we're aware of our sins, the more we need to reach out to Jesus every day. And the more we reach out for His grace, the fuller we become and the more grace we have to give others. As we do, His sacrifice grows more powerful and significant within us.

Today I'm coming to experience Psalm 32:2 in an even more personal way, where it tells me: *"Blessed is the man whose sin the LORD does not count against him and in whose spirit is no deceit."*

Bottom line: That kind of blessing described in this psalm is only available to us through the atoning sacrifice of Jesus on the cross. It's only through Jesus that we're counted righteous, only through His blood. As Christians we know His sacrifice paid the price that was due for our sin. Amen!

2—Cutting through the fog to a God that takes pleasure in us

Does this make any sense to you, or does it still sound like a lot of religious jargon? If you're born again (meaning a spiritual birth), you receive God's grace through His Son, Jesus. As we continually seek and receive the grace of Jesus, we confirm God's mercy. And this totally pleases God.

But don't just take my word for it. Here's what one of the most beautiful passages in the Bible has to say about our new life in Christ: *"For he chose us in him before the creation of the world to be holy and blameless in his sight. In love he predestined us to be adopted as his sons through Jesus Christ, in accordance with his pleasure and will—to the praise of his glorious grace, which he has freely given us in the One he loves."* (Ephesians 1:4-6)

I love the part where it says His grace is freely given and it pleasured Him. We didn't have to pay for it. Well, we wouldn't have been able to, anyway. Finishing the passage in Ephesians: *"In him we have redemption through his blood, the forgiveness of sins, in accordance with the riches of God's grace that he lavished on us with all wisdom and understanding. And he made known to us the mystery of his will according to his good pleasure, which he purposed in Christ..."* (Ephesians 1:7-9)

3—The victorious Christian life

If you can imagine the Christian life as a metaphor, look at it as a race under God's grace. Paul says it in 1 Corinthians: *"Do you not know that in a race all the runners run, but only one gets the prize? Run in such a way as to get the prize. Everyone who competes in the games goes into strict training. They do it to get a crown that will not last; but we do it to get a crown that will last forever."* (1 Corinthians 9:24-25)

And this is winning: Being able to say "I am not a slave to sin or sin's guilt. Instead I live by His grace." Check out chapters seven and eight in the book of Romans to better understand what I mean about freedom and the removal of guilt and worry.

As Christians we're free, we're a work in progress, and I thank

God He doesn't expect us to be perfect. That's why Jesus was sent to this world, after all. As Ephesians 2 reminds us, *"For we are God's workmanship, created in Christ Jesus to do good works, which God prepared in advance for us to do."* (Ephesians 2:10)

So we step out in grace, secure in knowing that God accepts us as we are. What other religion can say that? Every other religion is based on works. Jesus invited us this way: *"Come to me, all you who are weary and burdened, and I will give you rest."* (Matthew 11:28)

4—Reality check
Great, so far. But if you're reading this book and parts still don't make any sense, please don't stress out. If you don't know the Lord, pray that God would open your eyes and ears right now to the life changing gospel mystery of Jesus Christ. Then back up and take a look at Appendix A, the part about coming to know God.

On the other hand, if you know you're already a believer but you still have questions about what you're reading here—again don't worry. Nobody understands everything in the Bible. Learning God's Word is a life process, really. The more you learn the more God reveals to you. In the book of Hebrews it says *"For the word of God is living and active. Sharper than any double-edged sword, it penetrates even to dividing soul and spirit, joints and marrow; it judges the thoughts and attitudes of the heart."* (Hebrews 4:12)

I've been studying the Bible intensely ever since I became a Christian. But I've hardly scratched the surface, and I praise God for that! Could you imagine worshiping a God that we know everything about? He would have to be a dead God for that to be true. Our God is alive!

5—One step at a time

So please accept the possibility that God is bringing you along in His time, at His speed. No doubt He has more in store for you, when you're ready for it. Meanwhile, pray for God's grace, that He would open Himself up to you more and more. Learn with other Christians. Stay close and be sure to worship regularly. And once again... be different from the world!

Here in the United States people know more about the President or their favorite entertainer than they do about the Creator of the universe. They place their faith in the stock market, their jobs, their net worth, the daily news, in governments and the usual things of this world—rather than looking to our Creator for proven answers to all of life's questions.

But God has given us a road map to Him, instructions before leaving planet earth, a love letter to live by. So even if you don't understand the Bible at first, be sure to keep reading it because it's God's Word and has the power to bless you. You may want to begin by first reading the book of John in the Bible. (It's the fourth book in the New Testament.) Besides prayer, it is one of the best ways to grow closer to the Lord. Then I recommend getting into an ongoing Bible study if you want to receive spiritual nourishment.

The bottom line is that we should always look to Jesus for answers. God has already given us everything we need in the Bible to know Him and live a godly life.

6—It doesn't end with you

We need to be spreading the Word, too. Imagine receiving an email from a friend who had died and gone to hell. The return address shocks you, because you'd always thought your friend was a good person. He even went to church occasionally. He donated lots of money to charity, and even called himself a Christian.

Now he tells you of the agony of being separated from God for eternity. And he can't even begin to speak of the pain.

What happened? As his friend, you'd never taken the time to explain what you knew the Bible said about the only way to heaven. You just assumed he knew, or you thought you would do it next time.

But we can't assume anything while people are going to hell all around us. Are we witnessing? Are we letting our relatives and friends know how God loves them so much that He provided a solution to hell?

This is the Christian life, full circle. Loving others like Jesus did, pointing the way to heaven. That's the reason we're here.

APPENDIX D

A challenge for you - Part 1
"Preach the Word; be prepared in season and out of season; correct, rebuke and encourage—with great patience and careful instruction."
(2 Timothy 4:2)

I want to obey what God tells all Christians to do. After all, the last thing Jesus told his followers was to get out there and spread the Word. So for some time I've been getting out there and telling people what the Lord has done in my life.

But first I have to admit I've never felt like I deserved to serve as God's ambassador. In many ways I'm not really qualified as a speaker, or to be preaching the gospel. Obviously my life is less than perfect, and plenty of times I just feel like there are thousands of better people out there, people who are better trained to be out there sharing the good news of Jesus. I really mean this.

On the other hand, I also realize Satan can use my doubts to try and discourage me. So I keep that in mind. And the fact is, because God can use anyone He chooses, it's fun to see what happens when we clear our schedules for Him and make ourselves available. Just the fact that God can use someone like me really showcases His power and shines more glory on His son Jesus. I love being part of that whole process.

It's important to keep things in perspective and to understand clearly who's responsible for what. I always pray before each speaking engagement that people would not see me, but that they would only see Jesus through me. I pray that the audience would go away thinking about how they might come to know the Creator of the universe also. I pray that God's Holy Spirit would speak through me and that in the process people would come to know the grace, truth and love of Jesus. I simply become a conduit for God's message.

I've been given the opportunity to speak at schools, including California Baptist University in Riverside, California. That's where I met Dr. Robert K. Jabs, a CBU School of Business professor who invited me to share my testimony with his MBA business students. During that time, Dr. Jabs also encouraged me to put my testimony in writing, which is what led to the writing of this book.

It doesn't really matter what kind of platform I'm given. At schools, churches, business groups and public events, I share God's story of grace in my life when I'm asked to participate. When I was interviewed on CBN, the Christian Broadcasting Network, my story was the same: "Before I knew Jesus I was dead spiritually. Now you can have a new life in Jesus too!"

It's all about God's redeeming hand, reaching down to touch lives that don't deserve it. I sure didn't. My testimony is just a foot in the door, for God's Holy Spirit to work through me. So I pray that whenever I speak I'll be of use to God, just like the apostle Paul did, while he was sitting in jail: *"Devote yourselves to prayer, being watchful and thankful. And pray for us, too, that God may open a door for our message, so that we may proclaim the mystery of Christ, for which I am in chains. Pray that I may proclaim it clearly, as I should. Be wise in the way you act toward outsiders; make the most of every opportunity."* (Colossians 4:2-5)

Even today, after countless times of sharing my testimony, God's amazing grace can still bring tears to my eyes. I can't help feeling overwhelmed at the goodness of God toward me for the huge burden He's lifted from my shoulders. I guess that emotion shows through when I speak. How can it not?

Here are a few student comments from my speaking engagement at Cal Baptist:

"Aurelio really influenced me in that I realized that business is God's Business. So many people try to get ahead by doing wrong deeds. Aurelio shows that business can be successful and you can reward and glorify God at the same time." ~Trevor

Of course, it all depends on what your definition of "success" is. But Trevor is right, and God's Word says that the Lord will repay us beyond what we can imagine for a life lived in faith.

"Barreto's goal is to help those who need help in the same way that someone helped him. Barreto has found the meaning of life and he wants to give the knowledge to anyone who is willing to listen. [He says]... When you come to our C28 stores, you're fed for a lifetime." ~Adam

That's what C28 is all about, and that's the sort of model I like to share with students. Maybe there's a way to expand that model to other ministries or businesses. If there is, these students could be the ones God will use to make it happen. Maybe it's you!

"I learned so much from just listening to Mr. Barreto and he has assured me that business is just my career choice, it should not become my lifestyle. God should be the one that I am living for." ~Dina

It's all about priorities. It took me over 40 years to discover that truth; I'm hoping younger Christians will see that truth even now, so they can begin to build a lifetime of ministry now. The whole idea is to meet and engage this generation in a way that makes sense to them—without compromising the message an inch. Isn't that what missionaries do all over the world?

"Mr. Barreto took my perception of missions and my preconceived notion of the mission field and shattered it. The mission field is here…"
~Thomas

I feel honored to share my God given story with these students, and I'm moved and humbled by their comments about how God has touched their hearts and encouraged them to share what they've been given, as well. These students know how much this world needs God's truth. They understand how people are dying every day without an eternal home in heaven, without a promise, without hope.

Our missions work is first in our families, at our work and schools and in our own communities. When I think about my hometown in Southern California, my heart grieves. You see, we live in a country of plenty. Americans don't lack material possessions like people do in third world countries, and therefore seldom see the need for God to help them. I have often referred to my hometown in Southern California as Sodom and Gomorrah.

The problem is, far too many people have simply never heard the answer to life, the good news of Jesus. Or if they've heard it, it hasn't sunk in yet. They think God is up there and we are down here and Jesus is the Son of God, but that is all they know—if that much. We run into them every day at C28. From the outside they might look perfect, but inside they're tired and lonely. More than that, they're spiritually empty.

But we don't give up on them. So we ask them questions like: "If you died tonight are you one hundred percent certain you'd go to heaven?" It's amazing, but most people we ask can only mumble a vague sort of answer. They're not sure. They clearly have no idea, or it's a huge mystery. It's actually a huge problem. They're a lot like I was, that day in the principal's office, when I was first confronted with the truth of Jesus.

If they allow it, we share the good news with them, and after hearing the truth many of them choose life. Yes! I thank God every time I hear of someone who has prayed with our staff to accept the gift of salvation. You may not believe this, but we have shared the gospel countless times in the past ten years, and seldom has anyone ever complained when hearing the good news of Jesus. People are hungry to hear the good news!

Of course not everyone has to work at C28 to reach out to the lost. And again, we can simply share Jesus with our families or friends. We can share Him at our school and at work. We don't need the gift of evangelism or a college degree in ministry. It doesn't take a lot of training to explain what God has done in our lives—assuming He has done something, right?

It is good to keep in mind, however, that the person we talk to may be carrying around a heavy load of pain. Life offers plenty of ways to get hurt. We can also expect a reaction when the light starts to dawn on them and they start to wonder why they haven't heard of (or understood) the gospel before.

It's possible their Christian friends—if they had any—might also have been way too quiet about their faith. I know the sting of that realization, when we realize that people around us knew the truth but never shared it with us. They may be quick to point out that we've spilled tomato sauce on our shirt, but how about sharing something that will change our lives?

Our country's media and leaders are afraid to mention God's name, let alone the name of Jesus Christ. It's no wonder people haven't heard the message of salvation. The apostle Paul didn't refer to Jesus as the mystery of God many times for no reason. Jesus is the mystery of God! *"To them God has chosen to make known among the Gentiles the glorious riches of this mystery, which is Christ in you, the hope of glory."* (Colossians 1:27)

So it's worth mentioning one more time. Please understand: We do not need to be specially gifted by God to act as His ambassadors. It is God's Holy Spirit working through us that brings people to the Lord. We just have to make ourselves available to be used by the Holy Spirit. We don't need to be a pastor or theologian, Luis Palau or Billy Graham. Because if we are born again, we now live and breathe for God's glory, not our own. We are here to praise His name as much in our work as we do in church. He wants to be an integral part of every aspect of our lives: our business, our school, and our family. We are here to receive His grace *and to share* His grace.

We don't have to be afraid when the Holy Spirit prompts us to share Jesus. All it takes is being available and obedient. When we find ourselves face-to-face with a person who needs to know more about the Lord, we could probably come up with a few excuses not to share the gospel, but I want to share how we *can* overcome those excuses:

But I don't have the answer to every possible question...

The Holy Spirit works with what little we can offer, and the He is the One that brings a person to the Lord, not us. By the way, the same Spirit will provide all the answers you'll need. We can be prepared, but we don't need to be afraid.

But I don't even have my own spiritual act together. I'd be a hypocrite if I tried to tell them about Jesus.

We all are hypocrites at some time in our lives. All the more reason to share the grace you've received through Jesus. Don't worry; only Jesus was (and is) perfect. Share the grace, truth and love of Jesus with others before it's too late. There's no better way to explain how God's grace and forgiveness surpasses how sinful we can be when we just give it over to God in confession and repentance. Don't listen to Satan's accusations ("You can't tell others about what you don't know yourself!" etc.) Instead, just obey God's leading. Pray and ask God to help you. He will do it.

If we own or operate a business and we're saved, our people should know where we stand. Or if we're working for someone else, the same applies. Given the opportunity, we can let our suppliers and customers know of the salvation available through Jesus. We can do this gently and with compassion, perhaps with a gospel tract, a word, or a card. God will create an opportunity if we ask Him.

Or we can use everyday situations God brings our way. When things go wrong do our people or co-workers know we're seeking the Lord's direction through prayer? When we leave room for God to do His work, He will amaze us.

As a business owner, do you provide a weekly Bible study for your employees? Or as an employee, do you organize one for your co-workers? That's a good no-obligation, no-pressure way to introduce people to the Lord.

Does the company's mission statement include God or Jesus? Does it glorify God? Does it put God first? Again, that's a clear way to open a door for people to see Jesus in our nine-to-five.

Remember, it's not our job to drag anyone, kicking and screaming, into the kingdom. It's not our job to formulate irrefutable, bullet-proof arguments to bowl over every objection to the gospel.

We don't need to be the perfect evangelist. We just need to be an everyday witness to the truth that Jesus saves. Anybody who's saved can do that. If we do, we then also have to accept the fact that God's way is narrow. Jesus said that *"But small is the gate and narrow the road that leads to life, and only a few find it."* (Matthew 7:14) That means millions of good and moral people out there will never reach heaven—even family members and close friends, perhaps.

What can we do about it? Pray for them. Share with them. Plead with them. Do everything we can to make sure they understand that no one gets out of this world alive, except through Jesus Christ alone. They can't earn their way to heaven, and they can't buy it. It's a gift from the same Lord who said that *"I am the way and the truth and the life. No one comes to the Father except through me."* (John 14:6)

If we are believers, what can we do with a flat-out definitive statement like that, except pass it along "as is," as clearly as we can? The grace, truth and love of Jesus are available to anyone who believes in Him.

And if you haven't yet turned your heart and soul over to Jesus, then you are ignoring His claims at a very, very high risk. Ask yourself if a gamble with eternal consequences is worth it.

I didn't think so.

APPENDIX E

A challenge for you - Part 2

Jesus answered, "I am the way and the truth and the life. No one comes to the Father except through me." (John 14:6)

A friend once asked me, "Aurelio, are you telling me that a loving God will punish everyone who does not know Jesus, that Jesus is the only way to God?" That's exactly what I'm saying, because that's exactly what the Bible says, and the Bible is the Word of God.

This same Bible points to a God who is so far beyond us in more than just one dimension. He is loving, that's true. The Bible says explicitly that God is love (1 John 4:8). But He is also a just God, and on judgment day the Bible says we will all have to stand before Him without excuses, pleas or second chances. Check out Romans chapter 14. At that time we can either stand on our own, guilty and hell-bound, or stand redeemed, acquitted by the work and blood of Jesus.

Simple justice? Absolutely. No one's ever been excluded from God's life-offer because they couldn't understand it. By design, it's simple enough for everyone to understand, from young kids to death row inmates. And in a way, we're all on death row until we accept the pardon of Jesus.

I know it's hard to tell people that without Jesus, they're going to hell, because the penalty for sin is eternal separation from God. No one wants to hear that. Still, it's the plain truth, and it's the only responsible message I can offer. It's also the most effective way to put the gospel in context, since one must first go through conviction before getting saved. No exceptions, no exemptions, and no short cuts.

Think about it for a moment. No one reaches for a solution without first acknowledging there is a problem. We can admit it or not—that's our choice—but the problem remains, regardless.

Here is something else to remember: Many times we offer people the solution of Jesus without first explaining the problem. If we don't first make a person aware of their sin, why would anyone in their right mind reach for Jesus, without admitting they have a problem?

How can we appreciate grace, unless we first understand what the penalty is?

I know we want to be nice and show tolerance because we don't want to upset anyone with the gospel. But tolerance kills, and the truth saves us. The gospel comes with a problem and with a solution. If a person learns both the problem and the solution, and refuses to accept the solution, then a person is in denial. I have run into this kind of people and my heart aches for them.

Do you know what I mean? Truth saves; tolerance kills. The gospel is about salvation to anyone who places their faith in Jesus, but to the lost it is foolishness. *"For the message of the cross is foolishness to those who are perishing, but to us who are being saved it is the power of God."* (1 Corinthians 1:18) If you love a lost person, then you will pray and share with them what you have.

Please remember that very nice people bypass opportunities to share the life-saving message of Jesus with the lost everyday. But be aware that good moral people go to hell everyday. It's my desire to plant the sense of urgency in you to share the gospel with the lost, because you never know if you could have been an instrument for God to lead a person to salvation.

Good, moral people go to hell each day because they either did not know the gospel message or they did and chose not to accept it. I'm amazed at how many people reject God's plan of salvation. And in their pride and rebellion they inadvertently chose death. It really saddens me.

I've heard excuses like, "I'm not ready" or "God will not forgive me." Or "God is good and cannot let people die." "I know God and He will not do that" or "I do not believe that." Or how about this one: "That is your belief and not mine." The list of excuses goes on and on. But guess what? If you take the time to read the Bible, you learn that the only way to heaven is not man's idea, but God's idea. And who are we to question our Creator?

Getting back to my friend's question, "Do you mean that if a person does not believe in Jesus, God will let them die and go to hell? God is a good God, is He not?" My answer to them is, "God is a good God, and that is why He provided a way for mankind to avoid the penalty of sin (hell) and that's through His Son. And God is also a just God. Sin still had to be paid for, and instead of us receiving His wrath for our sin, God's own Son Jesus took the wrath for us!" Do you get it?

During Noah's time, hundreds of thousands of people died in the great flood, while only eight people survived. Read more details in Genesis chapters six through nine. What's sad is that while there was room on the boat for more people, only eight people believed in God enough to place their lives in His hands and accept His protection.

Today God doesn't ask us to step on a big boat to save our lives, but the concept is still the same. Now God has worked out a permanent solution for our sin problem, and He offers it to anyone who would claim it and believe in Jesus. That's what I mean by a just God. Here is a God who truly goes out of His way to save those who love Him and obey Him. Yet the reality is that most people *do not* love Him or obey Him. Why not? Simple neglect, maybe? More than likely it's pride.

Again, it's very tough for people to admit they're at fault, that their lives are broken and they need God to fix it for them. How many times have we heard, "I haven't killed anyone, I haven't robbed a bank, I don't lie/steal/cheat/etc." Or another one, "Surely I've done more good than bad." Really? Again, it's pride. We don't want to admit that we can't make it on our own. Instead we want to pick and choose our religion, and the books on pop spirituality don't usually include a chapter on sin.

Pride. Look for it at the root of misunderstanding, of trouble, of evil.

Pride—the root of every sin.

We believe in governments, we believe employers, we believe history books, we believe in our accomplishments, we believe in our bank accounts. But we fail to believe in the One who has the power to throw our souls into hell. Jesus said in Luke 12:5 *"But I will show you whom you should fear: Fear him who, after the killing of the body, has power to throw you into hell. Yes, I tell you, fear him."*

This is so scary. My heart goes out to those who do not know Jesus. Do you know Jesus? Is He your Lord and Savior? If not, go to Him right now! That said, whenever we hear that small voice leading us to share the good news of Jesus, we need to realize it's the Holy Spirit. God doesn't normally shout in these cases, so we need to turn the radio down, shut up and listen. When we start to hear God whisper, that's the time to pay close attention and follow directions.

In fact, next time you hear that small voice—the Holy Spirit prompting you to share Jesus with someone—just do it. Don't wait for a freeway sign with directions. Quickly pray first (you may only have a few seconds), then share! I know that not everyone has the gift of evangelism—being out there in the front lines, daring the world to believe. But I challenge everyone who will listen (Christians, I mean) to find their gift—their God given talent—and unwrap it for use. Let's keep praying for God's direction, and making ourselves available. Let's say 'yes' to God.

Use the particular gifts God has given you, and multiply what He has already given you. *"If it is serving, let him serve; if it is teaching, let him teach; if it is encouraging, let him encourage; if it is contributing to the needs of others, let him give generously; if it is leadership, let him govern diligently; if it is showing mercy, let him do it cheerfully."* (Romans 12:7-8)

Wherever you serve God, He will use you to actually make a difference in someone's life—maybe in the lives of family and friends or maybe in the lives of total strangers. We all start by loving people the same way Jesus loves us. There's a perfect model, right? We don't have to guess at the approach; He gives us so many ways to reach out.

Here are some ideas for you to think about how God may be calling you to serve Him: Use your financial resources for the kingdom. Put your money to work for an eternal kingdom. You can help a person in need. They're never hard to find. Maybe your gift is prayer, and the cost is simply your time. You'll never lack people and needs to lift up to God's throne. Pray by yourself, pray with others, but pray! Or use your gifts of service to help at church or a homeless ministry.

Whatever the calling is, our job is to trust Him; His job is to bring results. And as we trust Him, we can know that God will only call us to do what He equips us for. In other words, He will open doors so we can use our gifts and talents. If we don't have the gift yet, we'll receive it on the way. I know this from experience.

We all need to understand and accept God's schedule, though. I prayed for two years for God to use me, until He finally opened the right doors. But *finally* isn't really the right word, because what seemed like a long time, really wasn't. God just gave me enough time to be ready. He showed me how His time takes some getting used to—as well as some faith that He's in control.

Be assured, though, that as we sync ourselves with God's timing, He *will* help us help others—because the God I know is full of mercy. That means we don't get the treatment we deserve as God's enemies, only the bonuses we don't deserve as His children. He's gentle, loving, and patient.

The God I know also wants us to get to know Him better as we serve. How can we be sure? Because He's pleased with us when we read His Word and pray. He's also pleased when we follow His example by forgiving and loving others—especially people who don't deserve forgiveness or love. (Who does, really?)

In the end, we know it deeply pleases Him when people come to Christ, and then it pleases Him all over again when we continue to trust and obey Him. If *you* believe that—then you must share this great news with others. There is no other option; it's not the kind of thing we can keep to ourselves, the way my Christian friends once did with me. If you love a person, you will share the truth with them: that Jesus *is* the truth, the way, and the life. (John 14:6)

To sum it up, once you are saved, not only are you called to share the good news, but you are also called to serve God wherever He has placed you. And God wants you to desire things that are in His will. He wants you to have a perspective with eternity in mind. Jesus told us: *"Do not store up for yourselves treasures on earth, where moth and rust destroy, and where thieves break in and steal. But store up for yourselves treasures in heaven, where moth and rust do not destroy, and where thieves do not break in and steal. For where your treasure is, there your heart will be also."* (Matthew 6:19-21)

Here's a good example of how we can focus on eternity: My pastor asked me to talk and pray with a man from our church who was dying of cancer. Dave was about thirty-eight years old, married with several children. Naturally I felt sorry for him, since doctors said he had only about a week to live. So I visited Dave, intending to pray for him and strengthen him. That's not quite what happened.

Actually, after spending half an hour with Dave, I realized it was *he* who had strengthened *me*. And as I left his home, I sat out in my car and wept—not because it was so unfair that he was dying, but because I felt envious of Dave. That's right, envious! This man knew beyond a doubt he was going to heaven, and he didn't mind saying so. He could sense the Holy Spirit, and his excitement was contagious. I couldn't help being smitten with that same hope, all over again. And I couldn't help wondering how close I would have to be to death to share with others so vividly the sweet fragrance of heaven—the way Dave had.

As expected, Dave went to be with the Lord soon after that. We still envied him. And as it turned out, his funeral was a wonderful celebration of life, of God's promises kept. Pastor Milton shared with family and friends the truth that had also struck me so deeply. "Dave was at the foot of the cross," he said, "and he could see a glimmer of the glory of God."

A glimmer! The question was, from where I stood, could I see that same glimmer? Paul sure did. As he once wrote, *"I press on toward the goal to win the prize for which God has called me heavenward in Christ Jesus."* (Philippians 3:14)

So that's my prayer, even today. Staying in the race. Pressing on. Catching a glimpse of the heavenly prize. And if I do get a glimpse of it on the road ahead, I have just one more question that needs an answer: How can we not share this glimmer of heaven with everyone we meet?

APPENDIX F

Starting a business God's way
What good is it for a man to gain the whole world, and yet lose or forfeit his very self? (Luke 9:25)

I thought I would share a few of the steps I went through in starting C28. Plenty of books have been written about establishing or running a business from a Christian perspective, and most include what the Bible says about business and ethics. I didn't set out to write another business "how-to" book, exactly, or a business textbook. All I wanted was to share my testimony of God's grace, and what He has done in my life through business. And if that can bless anyone, then praise be to God! Having said this, one book I want to mention that has greatly influenced me in business is *Loving Monday: Succeeding in Business Without Selling Your Soul.* God used this book (among others) to guide me into what is now C28 and NOTW.

Sometimes it helps to hear it from someone who has made countless mistakes—and learned to trust God through the tougher times. Please also know that the more I learn, the more I realize I know very little, and this leads me to trust in my sovereign God even more. I can say with the writer of Proverbs that... *"I am the most ignorant of men; I do not have a man's understanding. I have not learned wisdom, nor have I knowledge of the Holy One. Who has gone up to heaven and come down? Who has gathered up the wind in the hollow of his hands? Who has wrapped up the waters in his cloak? Who has established all the ends of the earth? What is his name, and the name of his son? Tell me if you know! Every word of God is flawless; he is a shield to those who take refuge in him."* (Proverbs 30:2-5)

Now for anyone wanting to start a business, improve your existing business, or simply get closer to God on the job, here are a few steps to think and pray about.

1—Count the cost.
If you're serious about starting a new business, or just thinking about it, pray and ask yourself the tough questions: Why am I pursuing this? Will God be glorified? Am I in it for the right reasons? What are they? Are my spouse and family behind me? Are they truly ready to support my efforts? Have I received enough godly counsel from other godly business people, from my pastor? How will this business glorify the Lord?

If so, great; the world always needs better ideas and better companies. But still, you have to be brutally honest with yourself. You will need a 100 percent commitment to God, your family and your business, or it will never succeed. Can you commit that way? Starting a new business requires everything you have: all your energy, your resources and your time.

Most importantly, are you truly willing to glorify God—and not yourself?

Pray a lot and think on it—hard. Because many times the price a visionary leader pays isn't worth the final result. So you sell your new widget…and grow the business. Fine, but at the expense of your relationship with the Lord, and or your family? No business success is ever worth losing your family or your soul. Will you be able to place God first, family second… and then the business? In that order?

Having said that, it's true that having your own business can be extremely rewarding, and the Lord can use good business people to serve Him in mighty ways. Just don't fool yourself. If your only aim is money, you'll be let down sooner or later, the way I was in my first two businesses. And that kind of fall is extremely painful.

2—Honor God with your mission statement.
Having a great idea for a new or existing business from the Lord can lead to wonderful opportunities, but having a mission statement with a purpose that honors God is always the very best first step.

Keep in mind what the Bible says about people without leadership: *"For lack of guidance a nation falls..."* (Proverbs 11:14a) The same truth applies to companies. Your mission statement can be a great navigation tool to motivate and focus your people as you face the daily challenges of running a business. It provides a corporate compass like no other.

A God-honoring mission statement can also have a lasting impact on people's lives, their families... and the ones they serve. How does that work? Most people simply want to know what business people are thinking. So this is your open door, as well as your challenge: Will you use that God-given platform for the Lord? Will your business lead people closer to the Lord, farther away from the Lord... or make no difference at all?

These kinds of questions should make us all pray and think, long and hard—especially if we want to be good stewards of what the Lord has given us. After all, being in business is a privilege that offers great opportunity and platform from which to share our Christ-centered beliefs. Why not be clear and bold about our Christ-centered leadership by sharing what we believe?

From experience I know that God will honor this sacrifice—and yes, it is a sacrifice, because taking this kind of stand does not come naturally and will most certainly make you a target for Satan. Even so, the writer of Hebrews reminds us to do good by praising and sharing Jesus: *"And do not forget to do good and to share with others, for with such sacrifices God is pleased."* (Hebrews 13:16)

So before you begin a new business or continue with your existing one, pray and ask God how you can glorify Him through your daily routine, as outlined in your mission statement.

3—Be a leader who submits to the Leader.

Great business leaders realize they cannot succeed without God as their leader. Great business leaders glorify the Lord. They challenge and take people where they've never been before. They're driven, they think differently, they solve problems, or improve upon existing ideas.

Great leaders maximize their talents, their time and their treasures for the Lord. They are not afraid to dream and to step out in faith. With God's help, they make the impossible, possible! Scripture says, *"...With man this is impossible, but with God all things are possible."* (Matthew 19:26) Above all, great leaders know where to give credit, and they praise God openly.

Sure, being a great Christ-centered leader is risky and extremely challenging. Sometimes it can be lonely, too. The air can get a little thin way out there. And though the risks are high, they're totally worth it when lives are impacted for the Kingdom. What a privilege to have a successful and profitable business that produces good earnings that can be used for Kingdom purposes. Glorifying God through business is a wonderful and rewarding gift from God Himself.

A side note: Maybe you're not the one to actually lead the business. It doesn't matter—because to succeed, every successful leader needs great leaders supporting them, like Joshua supported Moses. In any supporting role, we have to make sure we can submit to the leader's authority, the same as if we're submitting to the Lord. That way, you will truly add value to this leader and serve as a great example to the organization.

4—Look to the Lord for encouragement.
Creating a business that glorifies the Lord is rewarding, but always challenging and demanding. At first, many of your relatives, friends and others may not see the need, the opportunity, or the connection as you do. Often people will question your motives or even the business model itself. That's why it's so crucial to look to the Lord for inspiration, guidance and confirmation.

Staying in touch with the Lord is 100 percent essential, especially considering all the doubts the enemy will throw at you. When we look to God for direction He will always help us! After all, *"...If God is for us, who can be against us?"* (Romans 8:31b)

At C28 we've made a constant commitment to prayer, and we've tried to encourage every coworker, supplier and customer in that commitment. It's made all the difference. We don't expect God to cover up for laziness or poor planning, but prayer reminds us who's ultimately in charge. Prayer allows us to communicate with God and hear back from God. It's the best way I know to have a dialogue with the Creator. Think about that!

Also, don't forget that if you're stepping into the enemy's territory with a business that will glorify the Lord, he's not going to welcome you in. Prayer for your business is your number one asset and protection against the enemy. Spiritual warfare is extremely real, so enroll as many prayer warriors as you can. Ask family, friends and people at your church to pray for the protection of your family and for the success of the business.

5—Lead through innovation.
Businesses seldom succeed without constant innovation, and

many companies are built around innovative ideas and products. As they bring greater success, innovations open the way to creating new opportunities and new jobs. Never forget that financial success is essential in glorifying the Lord and funding our ministries.

That means we need to ask ourselves: Is this new idea worth the trouble? Did we really come up with a better product or service? And if we did, are we sure the customer will be able to understand, appreciate or value this unique product or service? Before you set out to bring this idea to the marketplace, be ready.

You'd be amazed how many companies fail before they've even started. Why? Often no one really needs or wants the product or service. Sometimes the company simply isn't competitive enough, or maybe the business model doesn't actually work. Do your homework first.

I often tell people not to test God by praying and asking Him to make things happen that should never happen in the first place. I am amazed at how, in the name of Jesus, some people will actually pray for the most absurd things to happen—and then wait and wait and wait. Sometimes it's like praying for twenty feet of snow to fall during a 130-degree day in the middle of Death Valley.

Rather, Jesus instructed us to be wise, to be alert, and to be balanced. He told His disciples to use their heads out there in the world. *"I am sending you out like sheep among wolves. Therefore be as shrewd as snakes and as innocent as doves."* (Matthew 10:16)

At C28 we've tried hard not to copy the look and feel of other Christian retailers. Not only do our stores look different, but the shopping experience is completely unique. We're not about our products, but rather about the message of Christ. A Christian lifestyle experience. We've chosen to locate our stores in malls, where we can meet contemporary culture head-on. That's what innovation means to us.

6—Build it on the Rock.

Any business is obviously a huge investment in time, money and resources. So we build it carefully, making sure we raise it up on the right foundation. A story Jesus told applies here: *"He is like a man building a house, who dug down deep and laid the foundation on rock. When the flood came, the torrent struck that house but could not shake it, because it was well built."* (Luke 6:48)

We build on the rock foundation of God's Word even as we seek Godly counsel and wisdom from others. As the Scriptures tell us in the book of Proverbs, *"Plans fail for lack of counsel, but with many advisers they succeed."* (Proverbs 15:22)

How to find this counsel? You can take a casual approach by asking friends and relatives what they think. Or you can take a more careful strategy by bringing together and forming a Board of Advisors or a Board of Directors. Either way, the point is to seek wisdom from other godly business people before charging ahead.

Understand that you may at times receive conflicting advice from godly people. Yes, that's a little bit of a balancing act, but that's where prayer comes in. Pray for wisdom and discernment as you sort it all through, as you discover the best way for your business to bring God glory.

7—Be the wise steward.

Will you make enough money to quickly make ends meet and then effectively grow the business? Do you have adequate cash flow reserves in place to withstand the cash needs and demands of a growing business? Many businesses go out of business not because their product or service was bad, but because they did not realistically project their cash needs. Be wise, be prudent, be prepared, as Proverbs tell us: *"Go to the ant, you sluggard; consider its ways and be wise! It has no commander, no overseer or ruler, yet it stores its provisions in summer and gathers its food at harvest."* (Proverbs 6:6-8)

How will you finance the business? Will you have debt that you can cover? Are you really experienced enough in this field or industry? Do you have what it takes? The honest answers to these questions will help you discern if God truly wants you in business—before you go ahead.

Which brings up the question many people who are starting up (or running) a business ask themselves: "How do I know I am doing God's will?" That's always a good thing to wonder. I look for the answers to three basic questions: One, am I obeying God's written Word? Two, am I praying for God's direction? Three, am I trusting in God's sovereignty for His plans in my life?

If you can honestly answer "yes" to all three questions, then most likely you are in God's will. That's it! Do not turn it into rocket science. Simply obey, pray and trust in the Lord. He will make things happen, and He will give you confirmation as you walk by faith. And no matter how hard the work, there's nothing better than when we realize God has us right where He wants us. Then we can know we're being a good steward of the time, money and resources He's giving us.

From there, of course, there's more to consider…

8—Ask, "Who do I serve?"
At C28 we realize we're in business to serve the Lord first, then to meet the needs of others, and of course to reach people with the grace, truth and love of Jesus. With that in mind, much of our more

detailed business plan can be written for us—if we first understand Who and why we serve.

For instance, at our stores we obviously want to reach a younger crowd with the gospel, so we're always looking for ways to connect without watering down or losing the integrity of the gospel message. That's why we've developed many of our own NOTW *(Not of This World)* products, and we know from the response when they "hit." It's all about the message of the cross, and finding ways to connect people with the gospel. Although our aim is towards the youth, we've also found that we serve a lot of parents and even grandparents. Our job is to show the youth a clean and positive alternative to the misleading stuff they find elsewhere. I love connecting all kinds of people with the Lord we serve. As one customer put it, "I don't get it, but I like it!"

9—Use your gifts and talents.
If God has called us into business, that's our mission field. If you are a Christian that is in business, don't ever feel like you are less of a Christian because you are not working for a ministry or a church. That would be like saying the Lord stays away from the marketplace because it's evil or something. Or don't ever think that there's no way to please God in the business sector. This type of thinking comes from ignorance and from the enemy. Please remember: If God owns every business (and He does!) doesn't it make sense that His followers should also be in His business?

Blame the Greeks in ancient times for actually separating sacred work from secular work. In their way of thinking, all work was split into two camps, and neither camp had anything to do with the other. Sacred and worthy work was like being a pastor, priest, or missionary. And secular work was like being a plumber, doctor, retailer or business person. You get the picture.

The problem is, modern Western culture (ours) has borrowed major chunks of their philosophy, including the separation of "sacred" work and "secular" work. We think like the Greeks, without even knowing it.

Yet nothing is further than the truth in the Bible. The Bible doesn't make a distinction between secular and sacred work. It actually calls us to do everything as if God was in charge… and He is! Paul told the believers in Colossae, *"Whatever you do, work at it with all your heart, as working for the Lord, not for men…"* (Colossians 3:23)

So whatever you do, do it as if you're responsible directly to God for your profit or loss. If you follow Jesus and you run or own a business (or maybe you're a company decision maker), ask yourself this question: Do you merge your business practices with your beliefs and values? If not, maybe you should!

It has to frustrate God to see so many of His gifted Christian business people merely clocking in on Sundays at church, then clocking out during the week. Sound familiar? Wherever we are, whatever we do, wherever we work, that is where God has placed us. So we bring Him glory seven days a week when we include Him in all our business decisions and family decisions.

10—Don't forget your witness.
It's always good to remember that God has placed us in our positions for a reason. Remember Mordecai telling Esther *"…And who knows but that you have come to royal position for such a time as this?"* (Esther 4:14b) It doesn't matter if we're the janitor or CEO. Do your friends, co-workers, employees, suppliers or customers know you are a believer? That's the first step. But there's more.

Once again, take a look at your company mission statement.

Mentioning the Lord or giving Him credit in print is a simple but effective way to give Him glory. From there, look at more active strategies. Do you lead or allow Bible studies to take place at work? If you don't, how much would it cost you? When things go wrong, do you pray with your people openly for God's direction? How about when your employees or their families are hurting or sick? On the other hand, when things go right, do you praise God and thank Him in ways that others can see?

The dictionary defines the word, *thanksgiving* as the act of giving thanks; grateful acknowledgment of benefits or favors, especially to God. We can't hide thanksgiving or keep it private for long.

Christian witness should also extend beyond the workplace. Do you donate funds and encourage your people to give their time, talents and treasures to the needy? Does your company tithe from profits? Do you tithe regularly? Where is your altar of sacrifice?

I once heard a pastor preach that you should "Live your life and run your business in a way that you do not force your pastor to lie about you on the day of your funeral." That's good advice. And the Bible reminds us: *"Do not be deceived: God cannot be mocked. A man reaps what he sows. The one who sows to please his sinful nature, from that nature will reap destruction; the one who sows to please the Spirit, from the Spirit will reap eternal life."* (Galatians 6:7-8)

Obviously we all come from different places in life, so we're all a work in progress. None of us is perfect. But God is always patient with us, forgiving and full of mercy. If God is speaking to you about being a different kind of witness, please listen—and follow through. You won't be sorry.

11—It's a marathon, so stay in the Word.

For most businesses, it takes five years or more to build momentum and profits. In the meantime, I know what it's like to put in eighty hours a week—and how much that can drain you spiritually, physically, mentally and emotionally. Be prepared for that challenge. And just as importantly, make sure your family isn't sinking in the meantime. It could be a long meantime. Make sure you read the Bible daily, I mean everyday! Bible studies like BSF International help me stay in the Word.

Remember, when we're down or exhausted Satan has a way of placing doubts in our minds, especially when we intend the work as a testimony to God. Watch out! Make sure you've laid the foundation for those tough times. They'll come. That is why praying before you start a business and waiting for confirmation from Him is so crucial.

And keep praying—it's your lifeline. The more room you give God to act upon, the more you seek His help with decisions, the more you wait on Him… the more He will do for your business. His results are always ten times better than ours, far greater than we could have expected and that's because God is all about mercy, grace and love. He's all about keeping His Word. When we look only to Him, we'll see how much He cares and how much He loves us. So it's always good to remind ourselves who is on our side. We're never alone no matter how much it may feel that way, no matter how long the race.

12—Remember, He is faithful.

It's hard to miss the common theme through these business principles: *Prayer.* Prayer is the most essential element of success for any new or ongoing business. Through prayers offered in faith, over and over, God makes great things happen. And the best way I have found to pray is to read God's Word first, because the Word is God! John writes that *"In the beginning was the Word, and the Word was with God, and the Word was God. He was with God in the beginning."* (John 1:1-2)

I wish I'd known this fact years ago before I started my company, Dogloo. I spent ten years of my life building a good company, only on the wrong foundation. And although it was a good company, I failed to make it a great company. I placed my ladder and climbed it all the way to the top, only to find out it was on the wrong wall! In other words, I counted on myself and put my faith in the things of this world to build a large company—but in the end I lost it all. What good was that? God knew. Even though I did not know God, God knew me.

And the same may be true for you. You may not know God at this moment, but God knows everything about you. After all, He created you and loves you. He has a plan for you. And He's just waiting for you to call out to Him… *"The one who calls you is faithful and he will do it."* (1 Thessalonians 5:24)

BIBLIOGRAPHY

Blackaby, Henry and Richard. Experiencing God: Knowing and Doing the Will of God. Nashville: B&H Publishing Group, 2008.

Beckett, John D. Loving Monday: Succeeding in Business Without Selling Your Soul. Downers Grove: Intervarsity Press, 1998.

BSF International, www.bsfinternational.org

Chambers, Oswald. My Utmost for His Highest. Uhrichsville: Barbour Publishing, Inc.

Harvey, Dave. When Sinners Say "I Do": Discovering the Power of the Gospel for Marriage. Wapwallopen: Shepherd Press, 2007.

Hughes, Bob and Judy. Love Focused: Living Life to the Fullest. Laguna Hills: Crossroads Publishing, 2008.

MacArthur, John. Fundamentals of the Faith: 13 Lessons to Grow in the Grace and Knowledge of Jesus Christ. Chicago: Moody Publishers 2009

Tolkien, J.R.R. Lord of the Rings. New York: The Random House Publishing Group, 1954-1974

ABOUT THE AUTHOR

Aurelio F. Barreto III is the founder and CEO of C28 Christian Stores and Not of This World Christian clothing (NOTW). Prior to this, he invented the popular dog house known as Dogloo and was CEO of this company for 10 years. He currently serves as a board member of CBA, Woodcrest Christian School and Haven Ministries. His passion is bringing the gospel to wherever God leads him. He and his wife Peggy have been married for 31 years and have three grown children.